D1092977

MARGARITA'S OLIVE PRESS

MARGARITA'S OLIVE PRESS

Journey on a Greek Island

Rodney Shields

Ziji
Duckworth

Ziji Publishing

Distributed by Duckworth
First Floor, 90-93 Cowcross Street,
London EC1M 6BF
Tel: 020 7490 7300 Fax: 020 7490 0080
email: info@duckworth-publishers.co.uk

ISBN Number: 07156 34402

Printed by Creative Print & Design (Wales) Ltd, Ebbw Vale.

'Among all peoples, the Greeks have dreamt best the dream of life.'
Goethe

'The land sustaining us seemed to hold firm
Only when we embraced it *in extremis*.
All I believe that happened there was vision.'
The Disappearing Island, by Seamus Heaney

'Nothing is enough.'
(Buddhist proverb?)

love and friendship

αγάπη και φιλία

to

Dionysius Stoufis for the past and the beginning
Makis Paganopolus for the present and future
Lambis Mouzakis for more than twenty years
Daisy for courage
Sandra forever

MARGARITA'S OLIVE PRESS

Contents

Prologue

Prologue

By Daisy Shields

Important talks are going on. I have been given pieces of watermelon and a big gloop of vanilla cream in my water. I squirm in my seat not sure why we're here.

'When can we go swimming?' I whisper.

My mother has her other ear on the noisy conversation at the main table. Flies buzz round their feta cheese. A thin dog sleeps in the cool under one of the beds.

'Imagine what it would be like,' she says quietly, 'to come every summer to our lovely mountain. To be a part of Greece. Daisy darling, your father is buying the olive press. He has fallen in love with it.'

But when you're six Greece is a beach. I return to my watermelon where I am busy arranging the shiny black pips into patterns.

This is my father's story.

Dionysius
Poems and history, visits and ouzo, dance

There is a remote village at the northern end of the island where mountains reach the sea. The houses in the upper village are built high on a ridge with views of a distant dark blue sea to the west and majestic landfalls to the north. Along the eastern shores the seas shine silver at sunrise. My friend Dionysius lived here. He was the first to mention the house that stood in an olive grove and belonged to Margarita; this rare outpost of unspoilt Greece was to become my obsession, and love.

'It's a wild place,' he said.

*

My first journey to that village dramatically paved the way for the adventures I was to have there. I had travelled from the far end of the island on a motorbike, with Sandra holding on tightly and my son Sam following behind by car with our bright five year old, Daisy. It is a long trip, of perilous hairpin bends and sheer drops, but still best done on a motorbike, open to the wind and the fierce beauty of the land. On that first journey to the scrub-clad mountains of the north, from the distant stretch of coast where we were holidaying, I had plenty of time for comparing this ancient Greek island with my world of management consultancy where I had thrived for years. Each in its own way provided an adrenalin rush and the fact that I could be drawn to both worlds was not surprising. But that was not why I roared through the last stretches of free road and towards the steep slope up to the village and let the front wheel of our motorbike rise, to accelerate up to the square beyond – just an error of judgment! As the bike rose there was a sharp cry and a cloud of dust behind me; Sandra had fallen. Immediately, as if they had seen it coming, two women shrouded in black shuffled forward to assist her and shout curses after me.

I was mortified to see my Sandra fall. I was responsible; I had not let her down before – at least not with such a bump. In all our time together, we had made each other that one promise, which we kept. I had once taken a taxi across five hundred kilometres of North Africa to make the last plane for a rendez-vous in Paris. Sandra was rising through the ranks of her university and could become vice-chancellor if she wanted to, but she too held to our promise. People said we were a good team. This time I had been careless and thanked all the Greek Gods, or those whom I could remember, when I realised that Sandra was unharmed.

'Kind, lovely women,' she said, shakily dusting herself down. 'Look, they gave me some liquorice. Not for you. I bet they are swearing to do something nasty to you. So should I.'

Although I am not good at admitting fault, I apologised many times that morning. Perhaps it helped to counteract the curses. Certainly I was blessed that day, though I didn't yet know it.

The sloping main square was quiet when we arrived on that first morning. Looking for a place to recover, we stopped the bike outside the only taverna and chose a table in deep shade. In contrast to our own exertions, a sleepy fly explored us each in turn for a place to rest. A few minutes later Sam and Daisy drew up in the car. Service was slow. Enjoying the quiet after a noisy and eventful journey, we watched a mule laden to almost twice its own height with hay, walk slowly across the steep square in the blazing sunlight. A farmer, wearing a straw hat, walked in the shade of his mule. Both paused at the village shop as though discussing what to buy and then, without going in, walked on beyond a huge stone archway, riddled with electric and telephone wires. Nothing else moved. Soon the farmer and his mule were level with some buildings at the top of the square and were climbing up again towards the church which dominated the whole scene, and they were gone. Still nothing else moved.

Two men had come to sit at the next table while we had been watching the slow progress of the mule from the taverna to the church. Easier to travel down from the church to the taverna, I decided.

'You English or parlez-vous français?' One of them was talking to us. I started.

'Yes et oui.'

'My name is Dionysius,' he laughed, 'and this is my friend, Giorgos.'

Dionysius had penetrating bright brown eyes. His companion Giorgos was taller and heavily built, with a more easy-going air. Both wore open necked shirts with long sleeves but Dionysius also carried a light woollen cardigan. He said later he didn't like draughts. From time to time he coughed deeply. 'I've never smoked,' he said, when he saw me wondering about it.

Dionysius used to be the *segretario* at the northern end of the island and was therefore a man of some stature. 'The Greek word is *grammateo*,' he told me, 'the public registrar of births, deaths and marriages – and the many other matters which need recording. I know everyone here, and many of those in the cemetery too!'

His English was good, but it soon emerged that Italian was our best common language, since my Greek was then much worse than his English, and Italian is a good language for making friendships. As I talked to Dionysius, Giorgos left the table and walked over to a low surrounding wall, which was decorated with terracotta pots and deep olive oil tins, spilling over with flowers of every colour and perfection. He picked some exotic pink fuchsias and returned to hang the flowers, like miniature Chinese lanterns, over the ears of our daughter Daisy. She had never worn earrings before and loved the way they brushed against her neck. She exchanged smiles with her mum as she tossed her head from side to side and gently touched the flowers in turn, perhaps to check they hadn't fallen.

My younger son Sam was with us, after returning from travels in Turkey and northern Greece but neither of our new friends was interested in anything he had to say; twenty year olds were not expected to make a contribution. Sandra was treated with respect and courtesy, not least as the mother of Daisy, but it seemed that I was the main focus of their attentions.

'Let's have a game of questions,' suggested Dionysius.

Foolishly, I agreed and was subjected to a challenging quiz programme, which started with a question about the opening lines of Dante's *Inferno*. Apart from remembering the legend above the gates of Hell, which was the second question, the opening lines were the only thing I hadn't forgotten about the entire trilogy; I would readily 'abandon all hope' if the questions continued at this pitch. The height of the Eiffel Tower, rivers in Africa, names of cities in South America, so many questions; but they loved the full resounding title of Salvador – 'San Salvador da Bahia de Todos os Santos'. Dionysius jumped up, walked around the taverna repeating, then singing and finally dancing his own version of a samba the name had suddenly inspired. It seemed that willing foreigners were good sport on a slow afternoon.

I was able to answer less than fifty percent of the other questions until Sandra was allowed to participate. Eventually I came up with a better reply: 'I'm on holiday here, I'll tell you back in London.' Fortunately, it brought the quiz to an end.

By now we were drinking lemonade and fresh orange juice. Dionysius was saying he was named after the patron saint of the island, like half the male population. 'The ancient Greek God of Wine,' he said, 'was also called Dionysius, but give me poetry rather than wine.'

'Do you know Solomos?' he asked.

I did actually know the name and didn't confuse it with Solomon, but that was about all. Dionysius continued, 'He was the first poet anywhere in Greece to write in popular or modern Greek. Here on Zakynthos, he wrote his most famous poem, *The Hymn to Liberty*, which

5

later became our national anthem.' He went on to explain that young Solomos was sent to Venice and Padua in Italy for his education, as often happened at the time. He wrote poetry in Italian, but when he returned, he dared to write in popular Greek, against the aristocratic traditions of his upbringing, which accepted only Italian as the appropriate language for poetry.

'He was the first to write poetry in modern Greek,' Dionysius concluded. 'He re-launched the Greek poetic tradition which began with Homer three thousand years ago. Since Homer, I think only this Greek island of Zante has had a poem written about it; by Kalvos, a contemporary of Solomos. You'll find it in all the anthologies. Then there's a poem about Ithaka, but that's about the journey there, not about the island itself. And there's Foscolo. You know?' Fortunately, I did; he was one of the great Italian romantic poets.

'He was born here,' Dionysius continued. 'His poem *Zante* is in all the anthologies. No other island is there. And there is an English poem, *Zante* by Edgar Allen Poe.'

'He's American,' I said.

'No matter; it's still my island.'

With that he got up and walked away, saying he would talk to me again after siesta; he avoided the scorching sunshine by moving sideways into the narrow strip of shade cast by the taverna and other houses on the same side of the road. He turned a corner and was gone.

I was beginning to learn how knowledgeable Dionysius was about the culture and history of his island and later whenever I managed to check a date or sequence of events, he was always right. During the many hours I spent with him at the taverna, I learnt much about the island, more than I can remember. Dionysius himself, I shall not forget.

After siesta, I was planning to raise a new topic of conversation. Houses. I was wondering if there were any deserted stone houses for sale, near the sea on this northern end of the island.

2

Island Search
Stop at the end of the island….

Young people have been used to hitchhiking through foreign terrain, in the recent past, meeting and talking with a whole series of different people of widely diverse backgrounds. Now, unfortunately, modern constraints of motorways and security have made such contacts more difficult today. But try a different approach, rather one of place than passage and suited as well to older people as to the young. Visit a village at the top of a hill or by the sea, in the mountains, by a lake, or wherever you want to be. Find a central square and a taverna where local folk can be found, and after a drink or two, ask about empty stone houses in the area, or even ruins which might be for sale; ask where an owner might be found.

On that first day, in the village, as Sandra played cards with Sam and Daisy fiddled happily with her fuchsia earrings, I thought of my new friend and decided to use siesta time to explore the village. I too walked on the shady side of narrow streets between whitewashed stone houses. Dogs slept in the shade and a donkey stood motionless, flicking flies away with his tail. Sleep looked sensible at this hour, but I continued the tour, taking bleached photographs in the brilliant sunshine. When I returned to the taverna, village life was beginning to re-emerge, refreshed and ready to begin the day again.

When the old *grammateo* returned from siesta, I soon asked him about houses for sale. He laughed, said something again about knowing everybody at the northern end of the island and started talking to some of the farmers nearby. Others began to gather round and soon a torrent of suggestions were descending on us. My wife's cousin has a barn in the south! What about Costa's *spiti* (house)? I have some good land on the coast and my brother too! My problem in taking the matter further was to reconcile the romantic with the achievable. But I was sure that in the process there was a fascinating journey to be enjoyed.

When Dionysius asked if I was serious, I replied, 'Yes, but am I realistic?'

It was certain that many people around us were keen to sell something. What it was and at what price remained to be seen.

*

We met again the following day and set off early, with a fresh cool breeze floating us down from the village, eastward towards the sea. There are places on the mountain top here where the Ionian sea can be viewed on three sides, darker blue than the Adriatic and clearer than anywhere in the Mediterranean. To the north east, high mountains rise from the mist of the neighbouring island; further east the coast of mainland Greece can be seen on a clear day and to the south, hills, bays, inlets and villages beside long sandy beaches. Directly below, where the land meets the sea, stands a ruined tower, built by the Venetians as a watchtower but later to become a windmill. This ceased grinding flour sixty years ago. Now it stands empty until some new invader, some restless tourist with an image of far horizons, will see it and decide that no other site on earth could make a better place to be.

The first house I viewed with Dionysius was a cottage with traditional yellow roof tiles and a large stone barn where goats were kept in bad weather. The empty cottage was originally used by people who came to help at the time of the olive harvest in November. Marinos the owner soon asked if I wanted to buy. Greek owners want quick answers. You want it or you don't. In this instance, though, I was unable to play the game. I was uncertain that this was the right property; we had hoped to be closer to the sea, so I suggested another meeting, this time with Sandra. This provoked incredulous laughter. What was all this about discussion with a wife? Why couldn't I just decide now?

'It's called democracy,' I said. Marinos arranged another meeting and walked away muttering, '*dimokratia*'.

When Sandra and I met Marinos at the taverna the following day, he slapped his thigh in much amusement and laughed, '*Dimokratia, dimokratia!*'

'Yes', said Sandra, without missing a beat, 'Greeks invented it.'

The Greek word also means 'republic', but I am sure that there was no misunderstanding, and absolutely no chance of persuading Marinos to adopt *dimokratia*, at home, in either of its meanings.

A few days later, at the taverna, Dionysius said, 'Before we look at more houses, we should visit your cousin.'

'But I don't have a cousin,' I protested.

'You will when you've met Iannis,' he chuckled.

Iannis was a great mustachioed pirate of a man, in his late sixties and full of laughter. His wife stood beside him, small, wrinkled, smiling and gentle. The names Iannis and Dionysius seem to apply to ninety per cent of the male population on the island and much confusion can result when names are mentioned without other references. But there's an advantage if you have a poor memory for names – use one or the other and you will be almost fifty per-cent right. In any case, this Iannis owned a lot of land here and although he did not have an empty house for sale, he knew of several in the region. After generous talking and drinking of Greek coffee, he took us out to walk over some of his fields and stopped beside one which was surrounded by a dry stonewall. He turned to me and said,

'You may be a foreigner (*kseni*) but you're a friend of my friend. I'll give you this piece of land. You can build a house here. No need to follow regulations; nobody will know.'

Dionysius was smiling; of course, he knew Iannis better than I did. I thanked him for his kindness; Dionysius embraced him and said we should get on with looking for an old house.

The next house was built high on a hillside, surrounded by an orchard of almond trees, with wonderful views of hills and a distant sea. The simple building had two storeys with ancient stone steps leading to the upper level, shaded by two large olive trees. It was a charming picture-book house and we liked both building and setting, despite a collapsed roof on the lower part. We decided to find out more about it and began my first experience of the Greek property market. Just a fortnight later, our endeavours reached a stalemate.

We discovered that there were two owners, both living in Athens. The one who owned the main part was willing to sell but wanted too high a price and the one who owned the roofless part refused to sell at any price. Under Greek inheritance laws, family property should be left equally to all the heirs, who may then divide it up amongst themselves. So an empty 'dream' house with a few rooms may be owned by five or six brothers and sisters. If you want to negotiate during a three-week annual holiday, you could find that two owners live in Athens, one in Adelaide, another in Chicago. Even if, by a miracle, you can start business discussions with some of them, you will meet the leap-frog problem, where a price agreed with one becomes the standard to be exceeded by the next and you risk being lost in an upward inflationary price spiral.

Eventually I was forced to abandon my attempts at foreign family relations. Instead, Dionysius suggested a new search, for a one-room building that could be extended with permission to build. After just a week, we found just such a site, high up on the mountain ridge and completely isolated. It was surrounded on three sides by cypress trees with a vast open view over pine-clad hillsides, falling away to the far coastline. Enchanted by the location, I returned to the village the following day for discussions with the owner Dimitri. Surprisingly, for he had been keen to sell, he was nowhere to be found.

I was greeted by the taverna owner's daughter, Sophia.

'He's hiding,' she said. 'He doesn't want to see you again.'

'Why not?' I was bewildered. Had I offended?

'It's his wife. She is telling everyone she'll kill him if he sells the house. He doesn't want a misunderstanding.'

'Did she say anything about me?' I asked nervously.

'Yes, she wasn't friendly.'

I didn't need a misunderstanding either. We were at the end of a month's holiday and due to leave. I said to Dionysius, 'Perhaps I had better go and hide for a year, and come back when it's safer.'

'*Sto Kalo*,' he said. 'Until next year.'

'Until next year,' I said, envisaging more happy hours of friendly search. The following summer, I would find the olive press, and come up against its indomitable owner, Margarita.

3

Olive Press

Dream of this place, but may only the dream come true

In November, back in England, I received a letter from Dionysius. It talked of poetry and of autumn on the island and made me long for the English winter to pass. Surprisingly, I found that his letter also contained prices for each of the properties we had viewed together. Clearly Dionysius was still talking to people on my behalf. He concluded with a comment on the isolated house up on the ridge. 'Dimitri still isn't selling.' At least he's alive, I thought, remembering the incident with his wife. Dionysius was indeed a good friend.

It was late springtime when I met up with Dionysius at his taverna; I raised my glass and thanked him for his enthusiasm, in memory of our previous journeys and anticipation of the next.

'If you were helping me like this in England,' I suggested, 'you would be called an estate agent and would rightly be paid for your valuable service...'

Dionysius laughed. 'Enough of that,' he said, 'it's good to keep in touch with old friends on the island. Now let's begin again this year with Spiro's house. It is just five minutes from the coast and I have heard it is for sale. I think this may be the one for you.'

I was not disappointed. The house stood alone, surrounded by almond trees on open sloping land and was indeed close to the sea. As we walked up the field, Spiro the owner, a friend of Dionysius, came to welcome us into the main room of his house. It was a traditional house and had seen centuries of domestic life. In one corner a domed fireplace had blackened roof timbers from years of heating, cooking and baking of bread. We were walking into the garden to discuss the possibility of a sale when Spiro's wife emerged from an inner room. She said a brisk hello to Dionysius and shook hands with me but that was the end of polite formalities. Turning on Spiro, she unleashed a formidable linguistic onslaught, taking no pause for breath or mercy.

Dionysius backed away. 'She says that when the time comes for her to give up her soul to God, she will do so under her own roof tiles,' he said. 'She is very cross that Spiro invited us here to look at the house without mentioning it to her.'

'Will he persuade her?' I asked.

'Never.'

I thought of Marinos and said, 'So democracy is not entirely dead among Greek families here.'

'At least she is not yet threatening to kill him,' said Dionysius, 'nor you!'

*

And so I continued to enjoy the hunt with Dionysius. Buying a house in Greece was no easier this year. As Dionysius said, one of the problems was that prices were so variable. 'If a property is a million drachmas in the morning,' he laughed, 'it could be two million in the afternoon. The price depends on how badly the owner wants to sell and particularly if he wants to sell to you. People change their minds for small reasons.' Yet with our own hopes, we were perhaps just as temperamental. One pretty stone cottage called the priest's house was too close to the road. Another had wonderful views of mountains and sea, ruined by telegraph poles. The widow's house which we had seen the previous year still appealed, but the sight of the distant turquoise sea was a constant reminder that a car was needed to reach it. The more houses we saw like this, the more I hoped to find something within walking distance of the sea.

After more weeks of house hunting, Sandra was beginning to call me back to our family holiday in the south of the island and I was wondering where my search would lead.

'Are we running out of options?' I asked Dionysius as we sat in the taverna. Already the midday sun was high in the sky, driving any sensible house-hunter from the open hillsides.

That was when he first mentioned Margarita's olive press.

'There is one more house,' he said, 'and it is very beautiful.' He paused. 'But there are two problems, or impossibilities, if you like. The first is the house and the second is Margarita. The house is in a wild place and stands on its own – like its owner.'

I asked when we could see it. Dionysius smiled and mentioned something about my liking a challenge before he replied, 'You're on your own for this one, my English friend! Just be sure that it's what you want before you tackle the owner. Look at it first. Margarita will not mind. I will leave you at the top of the mountain, where the footpath starts.'

*

The track was shaded by olive trees and I walked easily at first despite the fierce midday sun. From left to right stretched a pale brown landscape, sun bleached, heaving up to the mountain behind. Below lay a steep valley that narrowed down a wooded rocky inlet to the sea. Here hundreds of silver green olive trees are planted in groves and clusters, or alone, magnificent and ancient, tossing their heads as they choose. The land lies open and gently sloping, like the great delta of a river, and to the distant right a high headland projects far into the sea, marking the boundary of this glorious valley. To the north-east, the island of Kefallonia rises, shrouded in mist, from the seas.

At first the path led me in gently, past sweet smelling fig trees and variously tinted evergreens of carob, pine and pistacia. Above the olives stood tall, stately, dark green cypress, first planted by the Venetians for use in building. Part of the hillside was intensively sculptured, with ascending terraces like a giant stairway, following faithfully the contours of the land. As I walked, I wondered at the exorbitant manpower devoted to creating such a work.

Later the hillside became steeper and rocks which broke up the path into peaks and troughs formed unfriendly barriers to everything except mules and goats. The next part of the track was more difficult to negotiate, increasingly overgrown with brambles and thorn bushes. I remembered this experience a few weeks later when I discovered that Greek maps call this untamed track, *dromo*. The word was familiar to me. In Greek – *dromo* – means road.

Unaware that this was meant to be a 'road', I pushed ahead, hot, head down through scratchy under-growth, unsure where this wild and ancient path would lead. Gradually, as if from the sea, distant and inviting, a breeze arose, the path opened out, I looked up. I had found Margarita's olive press. A motionless cascade of three low and interconnected stone houses clung to the hillside. Faded blue shuttered windows and grey stone walls gave the effect of a fortress battened down defensively against marauders or pirates up from the coast. The great upper house stretched across a higher terrace, partially screened by two great olive trees. On the left, a fourth, separate house projected out towards me, completing an open-ended U shape, facing the sea and the Eastern horizon. Close by, and a short way downhill, was another deserted stone house, separate but still part of the hamlet, like a small member of the family making his own way. I turned and stretched out my arms; the horizon of sea and sky reached beyond my grasp.

The first doors I came to were magnificent double doors, seven feet high, marking the entrance to the olive press. Between this building and the smaller house, I could see holes chiselled into the stone walls at the top and bottom of low stone steps, designed for tethering mules or donkeys while their loads of olives were carried into the press. The back of the olive press was built deep into the hillside so that the roof stood a mere two feet above ground level. I sat against the great house on wide stone seats, hand hewn from the mountain for the purpose. There I was cooled again by a rising breeze, deafened by the clacking cicadas and the absolute silence when they paused. An unseen hand would conduct them all to an abrupt halt and simultaneously they would begin again, drowning the song of the many little grey birds that sped secretly between the branches of almond and olive trees.

So this was Margarita's house. It was still and majestic with barely any sign of habitation remaining; a rusted petrol can, wire mesh against one of the windows and ramshackle corrugated iron – the modern replacement for slipped tiles. Strangely, these details served only to enhance the quiet magic of the place, waiting patiently to be brought back to life, yet already very full of it. Looking up at an olive tree above me, I saw a horizontal branch, a wonderful spot for a swing...

Dionysius believed that Margarita wanted to sell. But such an idea was poetry, not reality. Of the countless visits to other stone houses on the island, this was easily the most tempting bait yet – and the most impossible. Basics like water and electricity were problematic and access an impossibility. An ancient stone water cistern within the olive press building was embedded deep within the mountain to collect rainwater; solar panels may one day provide sufficient power, but there was no way that cars, motorbikes, tractors or anything on wheels would be able to gain access. This *dromo* would need to accommodate more than mules if massive amounts of cement, sand and timber were to reach the house.

It was three in the afternoon when I began the climb back. Never take on a mid-summer Greek hillside at this hour. By the time I reached the top, a search party was being discussed. Dionysius, my wife Sandra and Daisy, who were waiting for me, looked expectant.

'It's impossible,' I said. 'Quite impossible. You can't reach it. The house isn't a few minutes walk away, it's twenty minutes climb down a rocky path and much longer to come back. The house itself is beautiful... very special. In a wonderful location. It's impossible. You would fall in love with it.'

'Yes, my darling, but have you?' asked Sandra. She was looking at me with her grey green eyes, colour of the inshore waters of the sea, which seemed to say no need to answer, just keep swimming... Will she join me, I wondered, *tha pas mazi*?

'We must be practical,' I said briskly, 'it's a great pity, but only a fool would buy a house like that...'

*

To reach the sea is a walk of fifteen minutes down the hill from the olive press. A further five minutes along the coast is the fish taverna, the *psari* taverna, owned by Pyromalis, another Dionysius whom everybody knew by his nickname Kokkinos. Later I always called him Nionio. He used to go fishing early every morning and then cooked fish for whoever came to his tables. This white haired seaman became a good friend; he was highly respected along the remote northern stretches of coast and for me was a great source of local knowledge. So it was he who arranged for a builder to visit the olive press one quiet Sunday morning, soon after my first visit there, an act of easy friendship towards a foreigner, but indispensable to me.

For the second time, I found my way to the little hamlet of olive press building and surrounding stone cottages, with several heavy iron keys in my pocket.

I had decided that an initial assessment would be worth doing, and an experienced builder would be essential. The builder who approached the house that Sunday, climbing carefully and watchfully through the lower, then the upper terraces, seemed to fit the bill. Margarita's olive press, however, did not. Following initial greetings he appraised the ancient stone walls and leaking roofs in silence. On surveying the enormous roof of the main house, he hovered at the doorway and seemed anxious not to enter the room too far. The basic structure and even the stone flooring, hewn roughly from the mountainside, aroused his displeasure. Eventually, as the tour drew to an end, I broke the silence with a question.

'So this is Margarita's olive press; what is your view on problems and solutions?' I asked, as we moved, squinting, from the cool darkness of the main house into brilliant sunshine. I waited. He seemed surprised to have been questioned at all and paused for a moment to view me with an expression of pity, disbelief and scorn. Then, muttering to himself in indecipherable Greek, he lifted his eyes heavenward and turned to head back down the mountain, never to be seen again, at least not by me.

Quickly I closed and locked all the doors and set off back to the psari taverna, needing to think, think hard. Events were unfortunately confirming my first reaction to Margarita's olive press, as far as building costs were concerned. As I sat at one of the tables overlooking the sea, Nionio joined me with a bottle of ouzo.

'There are many building problems,' I said.

'I thought so.' He lifted his glass to clink mine, '*Yeia sou* – your health.'

That was the first ouzo. I am not sure how many more we drank, except that it was many, before the subject of Margarita's olive press surfaced again.

'There are others too, you know,' Nionio said casually. He paused. 'Margarita has family. They too own parts of the house.'

'I don't understand,' I said, fighting the warm haze of too much ouzo. I was apprehensive. And I did understand: if he's right, ownership of the property was split, room-by-room. That's simple. That's impossible.

'There's Iannis who owns the village grocery and Maria who lives in Athens. They both own several parts. There are probably five or six separate legal parts.'

I frowned. 'It would be difficult to negotiate a purchase contract with three different people – and one of them doesn't even live here,' I said.

Nionio shrugged. 'It's tradition,' he said simply. 'The family home is always divided up among the children.'

Six parts, three owners, millions needed for building restoration and no way of getting there, no water or power supply and heaven knows how many farmers' land to negotiate for access. As I sipped my ouzo, I could hear the sound of the sea on the rocks below the taverna. I heard the cicadas around the Margarita house and the silence. I listened to winter rain falling on the roof and watched the water flowing along stone channels to the *sterna*. From my left hand to my right, I could now touch the horizon of sea and sky.

'I would dream about that place,' I said to Nionio.

'Yes. That's the best thing you can do with it.' He smiled.

4

Meeting Margarita
House hunting succeeds, like success, by obsession

I had now visited Margarita's olive press twice. I had confronted the first of Dionysius' impossibilities and was captivated; now, a week later, I was to meet the second. Having already seen the olive press and had an initial assessment – if you can call it that – from the uninterested builder the previous Sunday, my feelings about this meeting were positive and apprehensive in equal proportions. Dionysius had told me that Margarita was well known in the village for her generosity with friends and impossibility with anyone else. This was all I knew when I first saw a figure in blue headscarf and skirt rounding the front steps of the church and advancing towards us down the sloping square. 'It's Margarita,' he said. 'Now is our chance.'

Dionysius made the introductions. Margarita had strong features, once feminine, now lined deeply, not I think with unhappiness but surely not with laughter. Was she sixty or seventy? I couldn't tell. Her eyes were pale and direct. She held her head high. Behind, the sky was white; must have been a cloud. She was unsmiling until she saw Daisy and hugged her tightly when she learned that the Greek name for 'Daisy' was 'Margarita'.

An urgent conversation ensued and the outcome was good. Margarita agreed to accompany us up to the olive grove. We went to find Iannis, a distant cousin of Margarita, who owned part of the olive press and piled into his van along with a full load of watermelons destined for his shop.

A bumpy journey brought us to the top of the mountain, at which point Iannis disappeared, leaving the rest of us to set off on our own.

That afternoon the sea was still and dark, but shot through with streaks of powder blue, like watermarks on a navy sheet of paper. Down at the shoreline a little island, locally known as the *micro nisi*, floated a short way out and centred the attention of anyone surveying the panorama in this direction. As I surveyed these lovely horizons it occurred to me suddenly that something was missing, namely the signs of human life that would generally characterise such land elsewhere. Dry stone walling marked the ancient boundaries of orchards and land ownership, but only one house could be seen for miles around, standing on the high rock that descended steeply into the valley. Other houses, if there were any, must have been hidden by folds in the landscape. The overwhelming impression was of land, natural, untouched and the sea beyond.

Preoccupied with the view, I failed to notice that Daisy's small feet were struggling with the large boulders of the mountain path, and was surprised to see Margarita pacing back up the hill, to return with Daisy on her shoulders. Both were smiling. Margarita had travelled up and down this track every day for twenty-five years and the extra load made no difference to her speed, despite her age. She had married the owner of the Olive Press at the outbreak of the Second World War, before her twentieth birthday. Her husband was then almost eighty; his first wife and daughter had been tragically killed by lightning, as they sheltered under olive trees, up near the village. As his new bride, Margarita would have ridden on a mule or a donkey, travelling slowly down the track for the first time all those years ago, guided by her new and aged husband,

and perhaps accompanied by a chaperone. Margarita surely was as fearless then as she is now, but not as fearsome, I hoped. I wondered if the old man, in such a beautiful place, would have recaptured his youth before he died. Certainly, neither this nor two further marriages brought Margarita children, a deep regret that she kept at a distance. In any case when Margarita became a widow for the first time, she was also left in an exceptional position, as a young Greek woman in possession of land, a house and an olive press.

As we walked along the pathway I watched Sandra as she looked up at the steps, the higher terrace and the olive press building.

'This is a magical place,' she said. 'You couldn't even dream of a place like this.'

Working its magic already, I thought; her word. I was secretly overjoyed.

At the end of the upper terrace, Margarita produced a huge iron key from the folds of her pinafore and wasted no time in unlocking the door of the little house at the end of the terrace. 'Be careful of the floor,' she warned and stepped watchfully across floor boards powdery with woodworm. Many had holes so large that you could see through to the room below and the adjacent lower terrace. In the dim light we could make out heaps of dusty straw and not much else, until Margarita flung open the shutters on the other side of the room. Cool air flooded in with the light and through the stone frame of the window we saw sky, almond trees and olives, and the sea.

Unlike the floorboards, the stone window frame, I thought, could last forever. It was well constructed, fireproof and no doubt earthquake-proof too, as part of a house that was designed to sustain many generations. Earthquakes are frequent on the island, over the years causing the devastation of almost all the old buildings, including those built by the Venetians. The last massive disaster struck during a week in August 1953 and hit the capital town severely. The timing was as bad as it could have been, the worst tremors occurring late on a Sunday morning, coinciding with the cooking of the midday meal. Stoves were wrecked and fires spread rapidly among buildings which had already suffered from earlier tremors. There were continual explosions of oil and petrol drums in the town and even explosions of hand grenades, which fishermen kept illegally for 'instant fishing'. The fires burnt for ten days and the blaze was watched with horror from neighbouring Kefallonia.

Apparently the British Amphibious Warfare Squadron, then based in Malta, had come to the island to help, a fact of particular interest to me because I had joined the squadron later that same year, during two years of National Service with the Royal Marines. Had I been given a choice, I would certainly have preferred amphibious landings on these shores, to the arid coasts of Sinai and Libya. Forty years on I was considering the risk of earthquake in another context, and added it to the list of questions that a prospective purchaser should ask, before committing to a 'dream' house on a Greek island.

'These houses have been here for hundreds of years,' said Margarita when I asked. 'They're built on rock. There's no problem.' I had my answer, and with Margarita there was no debate. So we continued to look around the first room, which was empty of furniture, but full of dilapidated paraphernalia. A grubby icon of the Virgin Mary was mounted in a flaking gilt frame and took pride of place on a makeshift shelf, next to a blackened oil lamp with a rotted wick. The room was littered with multicoloured pieces of cloth, rusted tins and decaying plastic bags. In one corner stood a hayfork that must have been in retirement for years. Margarita told me that this was the room that she had once occupied with her husband and I considered how life there might have been, and could be again. I was quick to assure Sandra, who had said little, that the roof timbers were in good condition.

Outside, Margarita was conducting the tour at her own pace and had just opened the high double doors to the olive press. This was the room which the builder had feared to enter; now viewing the roof again I was amazed at the enormous width it spanned. On one side of the room stood a large stone fireplace and baking oven without a chimney, which had blackened the roof timbers with centuries of smoke and soot. Great cracks in the wood threatened the strength of some of the main beams; others sagged ominously with age and weariness. But the roof had lasted for hundreds of years, and would surely continue to do so, I told myself, and Sandra. Beside the fireplace stood an impressive circular structure of stone blocks. This was the cistern, the *sterna*, designed to store rainwater collected from the roof. Margarita lifted the wooden lid and gestured inside. We looked down into a deep black hole. I picked up a small stone and dropped it. There was silence for a moment and then, far below, the clatter of stone striking rock.

'No water?' I asked Margarita. The slightest hesitation and then,

'The animals have drunk it.'

It was a clever answer. I didn't ask whether these were little animals climbing in and out for water, or whether local people take out water for goats and mules, but later I discovered that the only external access to the *sterna* was so overgrown that it couldn't have been used for years.

The walls of the room were almost a metre thick and the wall behind the sterna was formed almost entirely from solid hillside rock. A great white circular grindstone, king of the olive press, had been built into a dividing wall, when the business of olive pressing died out and the great room was separated into two parts for reasons of inheritance. A smaller stone, which collected the oil, was also incorporated into the wall, closer to the door. The family olive business operated up to about the 1920s, until it was no longer economical to press olives on a small scale. From then on, olives would be taken down, after harvesting, to a larger press in the village which operates to this day.

Looking at the size of the great stone, easily six feet wide, I wondered how it had arrived at the house. Nobody could say exactly how it happened; some said that mules must have been used, others that a stout cypress tree trunk was placed through the hole in the centre of the stone with ten men on each side, to move it a few centimetres at a time, down the rocky track. I wondered what happened at the narrow points of the track where there was no space for twenty men to hold the stone. There must have been steady nerves that day, or perhaps for several days. This stone was a major investment. If it had broken loose and set off on its own accord down the mule track towards the Ionian, nothing could have stopped it and certain disaster would have followed; years of savings would have been irretrievably lost. But having finally got the stone to the lower terrace, how did they get it up the steps and into the room? This mammoth task made our own seem less impossible. The Gods must have been on their side and hopefully would be on ours, if ever we got that far.

The room beyond the dividing wall was owned by Iannis and since he had left us at the top of the mountain we were unable to get in. I looked through some gaps in the door and saw a rocky wilderness with a straw covered sleeping platform hanging from the roof.

'People sleep there when they come to help in the olive harvest,' said Margarita.

The little house by the steps to the upper terrace also belonged to Iannis but I was determined to see inside and managed to climb up and look through a window at the front. Through the darkness, I could see an internal wall with a door, which must have led to a rear room. Like the olive press, this was also built into the hillside. I wondered whether the floor of the back room was level but Margarita didn't know or wouldn't say. She was too busy collecting a bag of green almonds and was now obviously keen to return up the hill, having locked her two doors and taken Daisy by the hand, up to the higher terrace. Sandra, Dionysius and I followed, getting very hot as we climbed higher. Some distance ahead, Margarita had again picked up Daisy and was carrying her on her shoulders. How well she could have organised a replacement grindstone!

The tour had been a great success. Now I was keen to hear Sandra's reaction. She had been silent for a while. 'What do you think? Isn't it great?' I asked. She paused before answering.

'These are wonderful buildings. A glorious position. I love the views down through the olive trees to the sea. Look at the little island. It seems to be resting.' She looked back at the olive press and added, 'Darling, let's go back to the beach. How could we ever live here?'

I had no answer and the question slipped away from my grasp, through the branches of the olive trees.

We caught up with Margarita at the end of her land. I asked who owned the land beyond.

'*Kseni*,' she replied

'*Stranieri?*' I asked Dionysius.

'No, not foreigners, just somebody else from the village.'

Later I thought back to this and wondered how we would be described by Margarita. 'Aliens', perhaps, or something worse.

*

That was my first encounter with Margarita. The olive press had lost none of its charm, though it was becoming increasingly obvious that the diversions of house-hunting were snowballing into one mammoth project. At least Sandra thought so. In my heart of hearts I agreed, but there was little I could do, for the obstacles were integral to the adventure and ultimately increased the value of the prize assuming, of course, that they were overcome. I was wondering about the third owner, Maria who lived in Athens and seldom visited the island. We hadn't seen inside the small attached house on the lower terrace, which she apparently owned and which had had been occupied by her family until her father died some thirty years before. It was an essential part of the hamlet, but family politics might complicate attempts by a foreigner to buy.

When we returned to the taverna, Dionysius and I discussed what we had seen that day. 'So what we have been calling "Margarita's olive press" has six legally separate parts owned by three different people,' I began. Dionysius nodded. (Greeks nod differently; side to side means yes, up and down with a flick of the eyebrows and a tut means no). Then he raised his glass and said, 'Let's look at the possibilities.' The front room on the lower terrace, belonging to Maria, was desirable but not crucial yet. The little house on the left and the great olive press building at the back were essential and possibly also the two-story house at the other end of the terrace. The *sterna* would be our only source of water. The next phase would be negotiation, to agree prices and basic contract terms with Iannis and Margarita. Dionysius said he would try to find out if Maria and her brother Giorgos, in Athens, would ever consider selling. I stopped myself; Sandra and I had never actually agreed to go this far! We both believed in partnership and of course I needed her alongside me on my island paradise, if I reached it. I felt I couldn't persuade her, even that I shouldn't. Practical solutions were definitely needed. Beyond that, only the place itself might persuade her.

Sandra agreed to accompany me with Dionysius, on my next visit to Margarita at her one-room house, which she now shared with her third husband. He was also called Dionysius, but to avoid another confusion, we called him Dennis. Not in Greek, of course! In his early seventies, he was large and heavy and slow, an impression exaggerated by comparison with Margarita. As we entered the dark room I noticed that a platform had been built into the roof for storing empty oil tins and rolls of black netting used in harvesting olives. There was a large double bed, which stretched the length of the room and a window overlooked the mountains. Dennis was sitting on the bed and gestured us to chairs. Margarita was too busy to sit. She had a fire blazing in the open bread oven, outside her house in the corner of a small courtyard garden. She was ready to make bread. The following year she was very pleased when I gave her an enlarged colour photograph of her stoking the flames and we shared a joke about it, *'Kseni sto fourno'* – foreigners into the oven.

During the week, they had been making cheese and Margarita was wasting no time in preparing it for storage. Lifting a huge plastic bag of home-made feta she put it by the bed in the care of her husband, as she searched for string to seal the top. But engrossed in the role of host, Dennis turned to speak with Dionysius. Disaster followed. He had relaxed his grip of the bag; it tumbled over the bottom step and an avalanche of fresh white feta cheese was spreading out onto the linoleum beneath the bed. Margarita was speechless, until she erupted into fury a split second later. I could only understand gentler words like 'pig' but Dionysius heard it all and unfortunately for him, couldn't conceal his amusement. In a flash she was after him too and soon had both men scrambling under the bed to gather every last particle of her precious cheese into a plastic bag. Negotiations with Margarita were thus deferred for a few days.

We were at the taverna, when we saw her again. Sophia, the taverna owner's daughter helped fluently with the translations; she told us that Dionysius was ill. His coughing had become much worse and he was at home, in bed. Margarita then started talking about drachmas for the first time. Unrealistic, astronomical drachmas, and how she would only sell her part of the olive press building, and not the middle house, at least not for the moment. Gradually the price came down a little, but we made no progress on the middle house and were forced to conclude that further negotiations would have to wait until the following summer. We were coming to the end of our second summer on the island. Dionysius was feeling better and he and I had a great farewell at the taverna, which lasted from midday until six in the evening, when I left very unsteadily on the moped, wishing him well for another year.

*

A year later, the first person I met at the taverna was Sophia, who gave me the news that Dionysius was ill and had been taken to the hospital in town. Shocked, I headed off to visit him and was relieved when I arrived, to find him sitting in a dressing gown, outside the main entrance, absorbing the last of the evening sunshine. He was surprised and pleased to see me.

'I don't like it in there,' he said. 'All my life I spend outside and now they put me in there. Whatever happens, I shall return to the village by the end of the week.' I smiled and handed him the book we had brought from London. Thankful for all the help he had given me on my search, I had often asked what I could offer him in return, and eventually, impatient with my persistence, he had replied, 'just books, any books.'

Now he looked down at the book I had brought, opened the pages, puzzled for a moment and then smiled.

'Now I shall win every quiz with foreigners up at the taverna.'

We had given him *The Guinness Book of Records*.

*

During the week of Dionysius' recuperation, I continued to think of Margarita's olive press. That summer, my beautiful elder daughter Lucy, then eighteen, was visiting the island with a friend and camping close to us down at the coast. She was keen to see the olive press and asked to come with me on my next visit. No doubt motivated by Lucy's lovely presence, Iannis was also keen to come this time and asked us to wait in his shop for half an hour. As we waited, we saw him disappear out into the back with a trussed bleating goat. Lucy looked worried and asked me about it. I couldn't reassure her. We sipped the sweet Greek coffees provided by his wife and made conversation to drown the noise, then the bleating stopped and Lucy was very upset. Little was happening in the square; a tractor passed through, an open delivery van filled with oranges chugged slowly up the slope and almost ground to a halt at the steep turning up to the church. A couple of boys on motorbikes shot into sight, round the church, past the archway and down through the square as though competing in the men's Alpine downhill; if the square had been busy, it would have been the slalom instead.

Eventually, after a wash and change of shirt, Iannis reappeared. We drove off on the familiar route, up to the top and through the panorama of the Eastern slopes. The road had now been surfaced with tarmac down to Nionio's fish restaurant, opposite the *micro nisi*. We parked near the start of the mule track and this time Iannis came with us. Lucy bubbled with her usual enthusiasm, for the house, its setting and the panorama. We couldn't enter any of the buildings, since Iannis had, as usual, forgotten his key and we didn't have Margarita's. It was near midday and from the house the blue sea looked so enticing that Lucy and I decided to head down for a swim, leaving Iannis to make his way back to the top. The mountain was difficult to negotiate and as we walked, we found the track increasingly overgrown with brambles and bushes. After half an hour the sea was nowhere to be found, the sun was scorching us, and we were forced to turn back up the hill. Our clothes were torn and we were scratched. When we reached Margarita's olive press we paused to rest for a moment. Lucy was still enthusiastic. 'Go for it, Dad,' she said.

Back at the top, we found Iannis waiting, and as we drove back to the village he confirmed he wanted to sell the small house and his part of the olive press building. We skirted around the question of price but he seemed to be hinting at a reasonable figure. Our best strategy might be to reach agreement on a fair price with Iannis first, and use it to persuade Margarita to be more realistic about her part. Both their properties were approximately the same size and Margarita might trust her local shopkeeper to have got a good price from us. Their surnames were the same but whether their relationship would help or not, I wasn't sure. Iannis shared water rights to the *sterna* with Margarita, but if we failed to get both parts, the problems of our sharing the *sterna* would be difficult. As we drove through mountainous hairpin bends back to the village I decided that our minimum target must be the little house belonging to Iannis and both parts of the olive press. The next step was to persuade Margarita and, of course, Sandra.

When we reached the village Iannis dropped us off at the taverna, where I had arranged to meet Dionysius. He was coughing more than ever but was charming with Lucy and still keen to make progress for us, suggesting that we visit Margarita and resume where we had left off the previous summer. Before reaching Margarita's part of the village, we came across her riding on a donkey with Dennis walking beside her. A chance meeting must mean fate is on our side, I thought, and approached her with greetings. But as we neared, she shouted out, and it wasn't friendly.

'*Figate kseni!*' Go away foreigners, we don't want you here!

Even Dionysius looked surprised and certainly I was. Lucy was shocked and whispered, 'Is she always like that?' Before I could answer, Dennis joined in and the shouting became a barrage. Dionysius turned to me and said, 'You're lucky your Greek isn't good enough for that lot. Maybe they are still embarrassed about losing the cheese under the bed, last time. Come on. Let's head back to the taverna.' We turned to run, and might have done with more youth on our side. Lucy stayed with us bravely. We were indeed pleased to reach the shade and friendliness of the taverna and had more than one drink together. Dionysius started to dance.

'Up to recent years we used to dance here a lot; a group of us. Look at the little stage at the back. Two or three times a week we used to dance there. This is the *Geranos*, come, try it!'

For twenty minutes he danced and I fell about. Finally he couldn't get his breath, coughed uncontrollably and collapsed into a chair. A while

37

later we returned to lesser realities and I suggested visiting Margarita the following day. It would be a mistake to let the situation solidify and worse to let another year go by, without result. Dionysius agreed our plan to reach a common price. Early the following morning he and I arrived at Margarita's house and knocked at the gate of her little courtyard, calling her at the same time. This time I had Sandra and Daisy with me, for protection perhaps. The black mongrel dog leapt to the end of his chain, barking violently.

Unpredictably, Margarita seemed pleased to see me.

'*Ela, Ela,*' come, come, she said. Dennis was sitting on the bed where I had seen him a year ago. After some polite exchanges, I said that her husband had really upset me the previous day; poor Dennis always seemed to get the blame. He sat silently, perhaps nervous of another eruption, which fortunately for us all didn't happen. She apologized for him, but not for her own more vigorous contribution from the back of the donkey. Then she produced a large watermelon to share and something happened which certainly I have never experienced over guest breakfasts in London, Athens or anywhere else. Having sliced up the watermelon for her guests, Margarita wiped the knife clean on her apron and proceeded carefully to carve out chunks of wax from first one, and then the other ear. The knife was long and sharp and she completed the routine without flinching. At the time, only little Daisy, who missed nothing, observed the ritual, and tugging urgently on Sandra's arm whispered, 'Please, Mum, I don't want more melon.'

Already she was learning that Greek hospitality made insistent second helpings likely. My seven year old had been more observant than either Dionysius or I; engaged in men's talk, we had both thanked her for generous second helpings. An hour later we left, with everyone friendly, including the dog – especially the dog, wagging his long black tail.

That was the last we saw of their dog. Some time later, Margarita asked the builder Andreas to build a new little house, an extra room, in her courtyard. The only practical space to build it was the far corner where the dog lived, so it was around that time that he disappeared. What did she do with him? No precious water spare, for drowning; poor old faithful black guard dog.

On the next visit to Margarita, Daisy came again and Margarita clearly enjoyed her company more than mine or Dionysius'. With her usual generosity, we were all given big chunks of feta cheese to eat, of a different vintage, I hoped, to the one which had been recovered from under the bed. Daisy was once again given watermelon, but seemed to have forgotten what she had seen on òur last visit and busied herself with arranging the black pips into patterns on her plate. The discussion kept returning to the question of price, which seemed to be softening, I thought. After we left, Dionysius knelt down by Daisy.

'*Micri* Margarita,' he laughed, 'every time you meet Margarita she drops the price by 50,000 Drachmas. Next time we negotiate you will come with us!'

I made several more visits with endless discussions and hectic travelling between Iannis and Margarita, who was oscillating on price like a roller coaster, but she was magnificent, and I wished she had been on my side. Eventually the plan started to work when Iannis agreed a price and stuck to it. Margarita refused to sell the middle house, but promised to offer it first to us, sometime later. With Margarita there was always a caveat.

That summer, when time for concluding the transaction had finally run out, Margarita agreed the price. She knew about brinkmanship. Its masters, in my experience, are Bedouin Arabs, due, perhaps to generations over thousands of years negotiating access to water-holes in the desert, where one error of judgement or weakness causes either terminal warfare or terminal drought. There was a time as a management consultant when I was a regular visitor to Riyadh, with a Saudi Arabian visa that lasted only two weeks. Everything serious or important would therefore always happen on the evening of the thirteenth day. I was dealing with a Sheikh who was unrelated to the ruling family and had no interests in oil. Fifteen years earlier, he had been living in a mud house about a hundred miles from Riyadh with practically nothing. When I met him he was thought to be worth the equivalent of about £500 million. This was very impressive considering he couldn't read or write Arabic and had no links with the establishment. He could, of course, count, like Margarita. My experience of brinkmanship and one or two other practical skills with him were instructive, but costly. I preferred dealings with Margarita at the taverna. I once heard her called the 'Arab banker' of the village. She and the sheikh would have reached agreements better than I did.

Our house search and negotiations now seemed to be at an end after three years. I told Iannis and Margarita that an engineer would come, at my expense, to draw up the necessary ground plan – *skedio* – and that preliminary legal work would be done in town. We could complete the transaction at the end of September. I said goodbye to them and turned to Dionysius who agreed that the odds of successful completion were still less than 50/50.

'Put it in the next *Guinness Book of Records*,' he said.

Before saying goodbye to Dionysius, we met once more in the taverna and discussed whether I really would ever have my own little stone cottage near the sea. Or was it all about meeting people, drinking coffee and eating feta? We had eaten grapes, pears and peaches; we had drunk the coolest water at midday, when only water is enough. We had met so many generous people in their homes and enjoyed moments of laughter. 'This is a good way of passing your life,' said Dionysius as we reminisced over a bottle of ouzo.

I thought of Margarita's olive press. Of the mule track, which in retrospect seemed less steep and long, of colourful rugs thrown over a tiled floor and of a kitchen with simple equipment and water. Everywhere there were windows and views out through the trees to the sea. The family ate together on the shady terrace; grandchildren sailed high on the swing; grown up children lazed in a hammock slung between two great olive trees. All around the cicadas sang and the smell of fresh bread baking in the great oven stirred appetites for the next meal. How many years away, I wondered, or ever?

'Now that you may have found your stone house,' said Dionysius, 'the hard work will really begin. You will have good memories of our search.' He paused. 'You will have to learn to *"prepare la casa"* my friend.'

'*Prepare*' spoken as though it were an Italian word was good enough for both of us. He often used the phrase and I think he meant 'prepare the home, be ready for life'. I would always associate it with Dionysius and never heard *'prepare'* come from anyone else.

5

Lawyer Friend
He is my guide, teacher, banker, lawyer and my friend
I worry about settling his account

In early summers we stayed at the Sikia beach, about a half hour's drive from the olive press. There we rented a simple room overlooking a part of the east coast that was peaceful and unspoilt. The bay itself is named after an enormous fig tree, 'Sikia', which had rooted near the shore line and grown almost to the full height of the cliffs behind. The branches spread wide and open and big leaves cast heavy shade. Daisy called it the magic faraway tree after the book she was reading and we undertook several secret expeditions across the water, with fruits and drink, to sit beneath and climb through the shadows of its branches. From the 'Sikia' beach we could see across the sea to the mountain where our olive press was located, at the northern tip of the island.

One morning, after Sandra and I had been swimming and Daisy was still in the water, we discussed our progress at the Olive Press.

'We're so lucky that Dionysius is helping us up at the village,' she said.

I agreed, 'But who will help us in town? What about legal and tax aspects, purchase contracts, the surveyor? We'll also have to find a public notary. Darling, I made friends with Dionysius; why don't you find us a lawyer?'

Within a week Sandra had found Lambis – a head bobbing around in the sea. She was keen to tell me about him. Was it her breaststroke or chance? I wondered.

'He has a house and family estate on the hillside behind the beach. He's a retired lawyer from Athens. I really like him and I love his sense of humour. Says we should meet for a drink at a local restaurant.'

So we went off to meet him; Daisy too of course. If there were ice, Daisy could break it anywhere in the world. I liked Lambis immediately. We had a little talk about this and that; he spoke good English, with a precise sense of humour. At this stage it seemed premature to mention anything about our endeavours at the northern end of the island, and in any case, there were many other things to talk about. Several generations of Lambis' family had owned the land behind the beach. He shared his house with three brothers and used it mainly as a weekend retreat; during the week he lived in town, in the family house, which had been destroyed and rebuilt at the time of the great earthquake in 1953.

For many years Lambis had worked in Athens and for a while had been employed by an international oil company, particularly to develop their retail expansion. When competing companies were involved, the legalities of retail site acquisition often required swift completion. I don't know whether Lambis always liked to do things fast, but unlike some of his fellow professionals in Athens and many other places around the world, he preferred to start the job while it was still being specified and almost finish it, seemingly, before one had time to thank him for taking it on. Lambis was very quick, but his eyes were even quicker. His eyes were disconnected. You would get used to looking at one of them and consider it to be the principal eye, until you suddenly realised that he was looking at you mainly with the other one. Once you have transferred your attentions to this one, you might after a while sneak a look at the first eye and that's the one that holds you in focus. I don't know what it does for his opponents, but if you were tempted to pull a fast one on Lambis, you had do it twice, once to each eye.

*

In town Lambis kept two ladies of his household, or his 'harem' as we liked to call it. He was unmarried and still sported a roving eye, though I am not sure which of his eyes tended to wander; if each were to wander in different directions, he would surely run into problems. Lambis was well looked after by his harem, the senior member of which was called Asimenie (meaning 'silver') and had been the housekeeper to the family since before the war. Several years previously she had been badly immobilised by a stroke and could only move with the help of crutches. Asimenie was very overweight and found it difficult to use the stairs; she lived most of the time on the first floor of the house. For many hours every day she would sit on the balcony watching people and traffic go by in the street below. For most of the day the balcony was shaded from the sun and for most of the year the climate is temperate, soft and pleasing. There are many worse places to be, of course, but compared with her earlier active life the constraint must often have been overwhelming. Over the years, I talked with her many times, but she never once complained of her affliction and always had a smile of welcome and a joke or a little laugh about something.

One year I returned to the island to find that Asimenie was dead.

She had suffered a heart attack two weeks before and Lambis had remained with her in the hospital before she died. He was deeply upset and so was Eleni, the other lady of the household. Lambis called Eleni the housekeeper's maid. She was small and wiry, always dressed in black, with grey hair, a pale wizened face and lively eyes. Asimenie had possessed tranquility, Eleni, vitality. Her hands were constantly moving, white, independent, bony, hard labour having made the flesh almost disappear long ago. Usually when I left the house she gave me a flower picked from the garden, a gardenia or a heavily scented white bougarini, one of several flowers used on the island for making distinctive perfumes. Once she gave me a honeysuckle.

*

Lambis and I met every summer at the fig tree beach. When the decision to buy Margarita's olive press had been concluded we asked him to be our lawyer. I walked with Daisy up the steep path from the beach, past vines and through an olive grove, to the great wrought iron gates at the entrance of his house, or 'The Palace' as we preferred to call it. Lambis had been resting, but swiftly broke into action and guided us to a long cool balcony with views, above the tops of olive trees, down to the sea. After orange juice and pistachios we discussed the olive press and I sketched a plan of the property. He quickly grasped the basic situation of five separate legal entities and three owners and summarised:

'You buy three out of five from two out of three,'

'Yes – hopefully,' I said.

'Shouldn't be a problem, provided the titles are okay,' assured Lambis.

Another of his good qualities is that nothing is clouded with problems until they actually arise, or need to be anticipated. I wish all lawyers were like that.

'We're leaving in a couple of days, but I could return to the island later in the year,' I said. Lambis paused.

'It couldn't be done in only two days.'

'It has taken three years so far,' I said, 'we can wait until I return to finalise the deal. A bit longer will not make a difference.' I could see he was disappointed not to tie it all up by the end of the week.

*

It was a bright morning in mid-October when Lambis and I met in the centre of town to conclude the sale. We arrived at the office of the *symvoleographos*, the Public Notary, to find Margarita and Dennis there, already waiting. Margarita greeted us impatiently when we arrived, immediately delving into a plastic bag and bringing out handfuls of almonds which she passed round. After we had all sat for some time, waiting for something to happen, Iannis arrived, looking casual and unconcerned. He sat down opposite Margarita. Poor old Dennis was already feeling hot; he found a handkerchief and after mopping his face and neck thoroughly, tucked the handkerchief into his braces, ready for use again. It was only nine o'clock.

Finally matters were underway and a contract began to emerge from the typewriter. Lambis said it would save time if I sorted out matters at the bank and the tax office while this was going on. Both Iannis and Margarita insisted on being paid in cash so I had organised the collection of large bundles of cash from the bank in Zakynthos town. As I left, Margarita was saying that she didn't want any notes larger than 1000 drachmas, the equivalent then of £3. Fortunately Iannis managed to persuade her that larger notes were just as good. At the *efforia*, tax office, I needed to find out how much tax was to be levied on the sale. In Greece, there is a capital levy system whereby property buyers have to pay about 9% of the value of the property every time it changes hands. The sum is not necessarily calculated on the purchase price, but on a valuation made by the local tax office, loosely based on the highest price paid for a property somewhere in the same region. There is an appeals procedure, but this usually takes too long to be practical. I went to the *efforia* to discover the worst, then to the bank to withdraw drachmas for the two parts of the purchase price and the tax charges. I paid these, then returned to the notary's office.

In my absence reams of closely typed paperwork had been churning out of the typewriter and the contract was nearing completion. Everyone was cheerful, except Margarita, who was talking to the lawyer at the typewriter. I could feel a low, volcanic rumbling begin to intensify. Then Margarita erupted.

'I'm not selling the olive trees!'

An intense and heated debate was sparked off. Margarita was shouting.

'I'm not selling my olive trees!'

Lambis said, 'You can't sell the land without also selling the trees.'

The man at the typewriter interrupted to agree that it couldn't be done.

'I'm not selling the trees.'

Then the *symvoleographos* himself appeared. Having seen the disturbance through the glass door, he emerged from his inner chamber; he could sort out this old peasant woman who was making so much noise. Matters got worse. Upon his 'authoritative' intervention, Margarita began to pack her few papers, biscuits and almonds back into a plastic bag, got up and made for the door, calling to Dennis to move himself. Dennis, who was sitting peacefully beside the window, rose from his seat in some dismay, and moved slowly after her.

'Help!' I would have shouted if I could have remembered the Greek. This was the end of four years search and negotiation; I had paid all the tax and my pockets were stuffed full of drachma notes which could not be converted back to sterling. For the sake of some trees everything was now at risk. I caught up with Margarita at the door. She was obviously intent on catching the next bus back to the village.

I said, 'We agreed you could come at harvest time to pick olives for yourself.'

'I'm not selling my trees.'

'You're not selling the trees,' I repeated, making a final judgment.

'And I want it in the contract.'

I paused. 'I don't think you can do that, but okay. Put it in the contract if you want to. I will buy the house and land. The trees will still be yours.'

Lambis and the *symvoleographos* came over and explained to Margarita that it could be written in the contract but it wouldn't be legal.

'I want it in the contract,' said Margarita. 'The trees must be in the contract.'

Lambis explained to her once more that it would not be legal even if it were written in the contract. Land could not be sold without also selling the trees that grew on it.

'I will never sell my trees.'

Margarita certainly knew about brinkmanship, but at least I had let her get as far as the door, before cracking; I would be better prepared when it happened next time. The remaining paragraphs of the contract were written up and everything was concluded with much stamping and signing. Margarita and Iannis agreed to give me the keys, up at the village, the following day. Lambis and I thanked the *symvoleographos* and said goodbye to Margarita, Dennis and Iannis, then made off for the nearest coffee bar down at the harbour. A ferry from the mainland had just docked and cars were beginning to disembark, adding to the congestion and confusion of the road in front of us. We ordered coffee and brandies. Lambis said,

'You couldn't have done anything else, you know, if you wanted to conclude the deal. If you had let her leave we could never have rescued the contract this year and you would be in the same situation again a year later.'

'What is the position about selling land but keeping the trees which grow on it?'

'It is a practice which sometimes occurs here,' he said, 'but whenever it has been tested at law, the courts have always found in favour of the person who owns the land. I explained to Margarita that she can't sell the land and keep the trees; it just isn't legal. She understood, but still wanted it written in the contract.' Lambis looked out at the worsening traffic congestion and shrugged.

'Maybe she wanted to save face over it. In the Ionian Islands and in many other areas of the Mediterranean, as you know, olives are of fundamental importance to rural communities and ownership disputes about olive trees arouse passionate responses. For years, olives have been the only benefit that Margarita has drawn from her property; I am not surprised that she tried to hang on to them, particularly when you indicated that you were not interested in harvesting them yourself! You have the Venetians to thank for that!'

He explained how they promoted the growing of olive trees in the islands and paid a subsidy for every new tree planted. Since Venice controlled every aspect of the export trade, including the marketing of olive oil and prices paid to growers, they were able to ensure good financial returns on their investment in olive trees.

'So for hundreds of years, Margarita and her predecessors have been dependent on olives for their prosperity. It may even have been your suggestion that she could continue to harvest her olives that finally persuaded her to sell. She negotiated it her way.'

*

Lambis supervised all the subsequent transactions. Because the basic structure of the property was sub-divided into so many parts and Margarita would only sell her stake to us piece by piece, these transactions have taken years to complete. Over this time Lambis' great ability with the opposite sex has had varying relevant consequences. When, several years after the purchase of the main house, we successfully reached the point of completing the purchase of the smaller room in front, we undertook our second visit to the tax office. An attractive young woman in the office was responsible for assessing all payments due by purchasers in property transactions.

'I know her,' said Lambis. 'She lives close to my house. I'm sure we can get a good rate from her.'

I don't know what Lambis had done to the good lady, or even if there was any connection with my application, but the payable amount that finally passed her lips was much higher, pro rata, than in the first transaction. She supported it by comparable sales in the same area and disregarded mules, mule tracks and impossible access as not relevant to the calculation.

'There's a right of appeal,' she said.

But we all knew this would take too long and be too costly. Lambis kindly lent me the extra cash.

'What did you do to her?' I asked him as we left the office.

'Well, it's not as simple as that,' he replied. 'I think you paid the going rate.'

'I hope you will be nicer to her in the future, in case of further developments at the colony.'

'It would be a pleasure,' he said.

'The colony' was the term Lambis used for our settlement at Margarita's olive press and, for all the invaluable help and kindness he has given to help it materialise, he for us is the 'Godfather' of the colony. He has never explained about the lady in the tax office.

A chance meeting one evening showed me again that Lambis was not a man who harboured regret. We were driving through the countryside past a well-known riding school when we saw him in the front courtyard. Sandra called out and Lambis signalled us to come in. He gave us each a warm welcome and ordered cool lemonades all round. After introducing us to his friend who owned the riding school, we were shown the stables and several good-looking horses. Lambis told us how he used to ride through here every day as a boy, becoming very competent and keen on riding. He continued to ride after being called up for military service in the army. On one occasion, his enthusiasm had galloped away and he had taken out to exercise the horses belonging to the General, without permission.

'They hadn't had such a run for years, but the General heard about it, and got very angry. In fact, he sentenced me to an extra month of military service, at the end of my period. I had no regrets.'

'My sympathies are with the General,' I said. 'Some young lieutenant taking his horses from him and riding them as he himself could never do again. Given half a chance, you'd have taken his mistress too, for a ride. Poor old chap. Lucky he didn't threaten a duel.'

'There was a difference with the mistress,' said Lambis. 'The General never knew.'

*

One year when we visited Lambis at his palace, he was out watering the roses. We had recently given him a glossy book about gardening in the Mediterranean region, which was a combination of beautiful colour photographs and sound practical advice.

'You've come to help?' he asked.

'The book was intended to help,' said Sandra.

'It's lovely, but it doesn't do the digging.'

'We're going for a swim,' said Sandra.

'At least come for a tour first…' said Lambis.

We started by the row of pink and white oleanders on each side of the drive leading up to the house.

'To get them to flower as freely and continuously as this, they must have water from time to time.' Then after taking us round the rose garden, he took us to a shady secluded corner, brought out some deck chairs and started to chat about the old days and the ancient responsibilities of his family on the estate. Meanwhile Daisy was following the trail of some pretty creepers winding their way over a garden wall. We saw her stoop down to examine the roots and suddenly Lambis called out urgently.

'Don't reach under the leaves and bushes, Daisy! We have a lot of snakes here, going after the water. Come and look at the ditch over here where the snakes enter the garden from the hillside.'

He walked over, took her hand, and together they wandered off carefully down the pathway.

When they returned, he explained. 'There's no effective way of keeping snakes out. Sometimes they even slither up onto the balcony and try to enter the house. I'm very careful. I have never been bitten, *ktipo ksilo* – touch wood. Now come and look at the old garden and the terraces of fruit trees.'

We followed the path over the ditch, past the wire netting fence and into the kingdom of snakes. Suddenly the shade deepened and everywhere was silent and calm. The lemon trees were heavily laden and we caught glimpses of smooth yellow skins behind shiny dark green leaves.

'Pick as many as you like,' Lambis offered. 'Most of the ones on the ground are okay too; there shouldn't be many wasps around. My grandfather planted these trees. He had more than twenty gardeners working here; nobody can manage that these days.'

There were big spreading fig trees, pear trees and vines higher up the hillside. Most of the ground was covered with a thick soft layer of composting leaves, a richness for the roots of fruit trees. A broken stone wellhead showed where once an important source of water was now superseded elsewhere by the electric pump. Terraces surrounded the central area but were not maintained, though good stonework demonstrated the quality of the original workmanship. It was a place where anything could happen and nothing did, except the growing of fruits and trees, and the birds and insects which they supported.

We came away laden with lemons, figs and pears. 'I'm sorry we haven't been much help with your gardening,' said Sandra, 'but thank you for the tour and all the fruit.'

'We'll make a plan for gardening another time,' said Lambis.

*

Over the years Lambis and I have become good friends, exchanging letters and seeing a lot of each other on the island – a chance meeting in the sea had earned us a very special ally, and friend. That special autumn, early in my relationship with Lambis, was one of celebration. The successful purchase of the main part of Margarita's olive press marked the beginning of our life there and a new friendship. But there was also an old friend I had not forgotten. I was keen to tell Dionysius the news before I had to leave again for England. The evening before my departure I drove up to the village. He had suggested we meet, not at the taverna, but for the first time in our friendship, at his house. When I arrived he was sitting outside with his wife, in the evening sun. They were surrounded by dogs, goats and chickens.

'We live with the animals here,' Dionysius smiled as I came through the gate.

'You have plenty of space,' I said, looking at the large field in front of the building.

We talked for a while and then he suggested we go for a drink at a bar on the other side of the field. I said goodbye to his wife and walked with Dionysius and two of his dogs. At the bar he sent them home and they ran back obediently, wagging their tails. Some of his friends were sitting at the end table, including the Mayor, to whom he had introduced me the previous year. The Mayor was extremely friendly; we spoke German which at that time was still much better than my Greek. The rest of them of course were speaking only Greek in a way which was still far beyond my capacity, though inside I shared their laughter and occasionally Dionysius or the Mayor would explain and invite me to comment.

Soon they all left and Dionysius and I discussed the news that we were now owners of the olive press. 'You must come in the spring,' he said. 'It is the best time of year… the wild flowers are so beautiful. You will never have seen so many, nor so many butterflies. We all look forward to it in the wet winter months.'

As we talked he became more philosophical. 'You must take every chance to do these things, Rodney. When life leaves you it takes the spring too; and the butterflies and flowers.'

We talked some more, the seasons, the house, the books to bring next year. Too soon it was time to leave, in the last of the daylight. I was anxious about Dionysius coughing so badly but he said he would never go back to hospital. We said goodbye. As I walked to the door I remembered reading that the Bushmen of the Kalahari desert never turn round once they have said good bye; if you should turn, leaving is too hard. I opened the door. The air outside was colder than within the bar and I shivered more than was needed by the change of temperature. Silently I said goodbye again. Greeks say *'sto kalo'* or *'antio'* – sounding like the French word *'adieu'*. We always spoke Italian. *'Ciao*, old friend.' I started the moped and left.

*

The mellow autumn, that at last had seen us buy the main part of Margarita's olive press, turned into a vicious winter. This brought with it death of the fig tree, at the Sikia beach, destroyed by frost in a single season. Now the great tree that gave the beach its name stands a skeleton, losing dead branches in gales and high seas, until only a trunk remains, before a storm finally pulls it crashing into the sea.

6

Place
Leave a structure behind and let it well be done

In January I received a letter from Lambis with the news that Dionysius had died. I still think of the last conversation between us. Perhaps he did find flowers as beautiful as the springtime wild flowers of his island. His wife would be returning to Athens and I wrote to her, including an enlargement of a recent photograph of her husband. Two years later I saw it on a desk in the mayor's office, in the upper village, where he had lived all his life. Good place for it to be, I thought.

When summer came, I began alone, as I had the first time. My first port of call was Iannis' shop in the village, to collect the key to the little house. While there I took the opportunity to buy paint and some tools, which I knew were necessary; the handover of the keys was only the beginning. I was particularly keen to find a garden hoe, vital for clearing vegetation from pathways and terraces, but nowhere could I find one. Iannis and I shook hands and he offered me coffee before I left. I was keen to set off as soon as possible, but you refuse these offers of hospitality at your peril. Eventually we said our goodbyes and I rode away on the moped, an odd assortment of implements sticking out in all directions, precariously balanced and lucky still to be on the moped twenty minutes later when I arrived at the bottom of the hill. By now it was noon and the sun high in the sky.

Ten minutes later, carrying everything up the hill in great discomfort,

I was forced to pause, under an olive tree, the first available shade. The tree is planted alongside the path, by someone who, you feel, knew about this walk. There is a rock upon which you can sit and admire the view. The heat of the day was approaching its peak; everywhere cicadas were clacking, olive branches glimmering and shifting in a light breeze. Fields around had been sown with wheat, now long harvested. A line of newly planted olive trees stretched further up the path, past a dried-up river course and over the other side. This is where the real climb begins and the path itself is lost among the rocks. Here the track is badly overgrown with brambles and thorn bushes, with which I fight a losing battle every year. Climbing higher, I resolved to minimise walking here during the midday hours.

Suddenly I was thinking of my conversations with Dionysius at the taverna. At this point on the journey it was natural that I remembered Dionysius' love of Dante, mentally altering the famous quotation to 'Lasciate ogni speranza voi che "camminate" qui' – abandon all hope you who walk here. I turned to look out at the glorious panorama. No, it wasn't that bad. Not that bad; there was paradise here. Ahead there stood a large group of tall dark green cypress, perhaps twenty to thirty, surrounded by a stone wall. Not a forest, a wood or a plantation. It is a cypress garden, where we have walked many times since. The ground is soft with fallen leaves and small cones. Looking down through the tree trunks, you can see the distant brilliant blue of the sea. In this lovely place, you could put up a tent, a deck chair or a hammock; smell the resinous tangy scent of the cypress branches; see small grey birds flit between trees; no people come here. The faint whisper of a breeze reaches up from the coast.

Looking up the hill, through the trees, to the higher terraces where Margarita's olive press stood, I caught glimpses of the stonework and the yellow tiles of the roof. It was ours – or at least three fifths of it was. I could hardly believe it. When I arrived I sat for a moment on the stone seats of the terrace, holding two keys in my hand. One from Iannis for the little house that I had not yet seen inside, and one from Margarita for the for the olive press building. Each key is nine inches of solid iron. I began with the one that Iannis had given me, opening the door of his house, my house, for the first time.

The timbered roof and the walls were black with soot and tar. The room had no chimney and over the years, flames and smoke from the lovely rounded fireplace and baking oven that stood in one corner had blackened everything. There was furniture, two wooden stools and a low table stood covered in cobwebs. But the floor... I wanted to clutch my head like the old builder. It was solid mountain rock. The walls had simply been built up around the jagged and uneven boulders of the mountain-side that now formed the floor. Leaving this problem aside for a moment, I turned to the door that led into a rear room. As I opened it a flock of brown bats flew at me, out into the main room amid much flapping and squeaking. The room was stacked with straw from the floor level right up to the cross timbers of the roof; only bats, snakes and insects could enter. I still couldn't discover if the floor was level through to the end wall.

Taking a deep breath I walked back out onto the higher terrace, unlocked and pushed open the double doors of the great olive press building. As they creaked apart, sunlight swept through to the far corner and I saw the huge stone fireplace and baking oven, the *'pithi'* – stone vessel for olive oil – and the enormous *sterna*. Compared with the first time, I now had a very different feeling as I lifted off the lid and looked down into the darkness of the *sterna*, my *sterna*. Again I threw in a stone and heard it clatter against an empty bottom. I had expected a miracle perhaps; a *sterna* full of water to accompany the first miracle of the successful purchase. As Dionysius had promised, I would need to work hard here. The *sterna* was at least two metres in diameter and another five deep, chopped out of the solid rock of the mountain. I imagined undertaking the task with a hammer and chisel. The island has rain only between October and March, so the first summer would have been the worst, then each year a little more of the winter rainfall would be collected. Perhaps after all, the hardest of the work had already been done.

Rainwater, falling from the rear slope of the roof to paving slabs on the ground, travels through a hole in the wall, down a slope, and into the sterna. Simple engineering. Later I blocked this channel deciding instead to take water from both roof slopes via gutters and pipes directly into the *sterna*. One day, it would be good to re-establish the original water channel and in the winter months sit dry and warm in front of the fire, watching rain flow into the *sterna* as it would have done for the last three hundred winters.

*

Gradually I absorbed the reality that all this was ours now. It was time to get to work. The first job was to remove two iron rings from the wall on each side of the door to the rear room. These rings had been used for tethering animals and would therefore not be needed in the new regime.

The first ring was attached to an iron bolt that slid out of the wall quite easily. The second ring, on the far side, was very tough; something was different about it. I knocked it with a hammer and struggled to turn it with pincers. Suddenly it came loose and out of the wall, attached to the ring, came a hoe! The ring was for a wooden handle and formed the top part of a blade, which had been sandwiched between two rocks in the wall for years. It was a good hoe and later I attached a wooden handle. The event was disturbing and miraculous; in the sunshine the blade of the hoe reflected the silver green leaves of olive branches, reflecting more light than the sun. I took another look; it was still only a hoe. Time for a meal and a swim, I thought. So I set off down the hill to join the road to the taverna.

*

I stayed down at the *psari* taverna and every morning walked up the hill to spend the day hard at work in the little house, removing the tar and the soot from the roof timbers and the walls, filling holes, replacing broken tiles and cleaning away centuries of cobwebs. I had already bought white paint from Iannis' shop but Nionio insisted that the best way to cover black stains of soot and tar was to cover them first with paint and then with a double coat of whitewash. '*Asvestis*', he said and kindly offered to get me a bag when he went into town. The following morning a bag of *asvestis* was waiting for me. It was so enormous that I could hardly lift it onto the back of the moped. I shuddered at the thought of trying to carry it up the hill, but there was no alternative. In short flattening bursts, I managed to get it as far as the first shady olive tree, where the bag and I collapsed in a heap. I left it at the tree and went on up to the house for a couple of thick plastic sacks. When I returned

I divided the original sack of *asvestis* into three equal parts, for carrying up on three separate trips.

Later I thanked Nionio for the bag of *asvestis* and mentioned in passing that it was rather heavy. Were there not easier ways of flattening foreign visitors? He laughed. 'Yes, I shall have to try those later.' In fact he never did; it would have been bad for taverna business and he seemed satisfied with trial by whitewash bag. The following year, Nionio and I were looking out of one of the taverna windows which open onto his vegetable garden. It was lush with tomatoes. Mounds of earth were lined up in rows, side by side and each about two metres long.

'Remember the help you gave me with the whitewash?' I said.

Nionio looked surprised, but nodded 'yes'.

'Are those mounds the graves of defeated taverna customers?'

*

My eldest son Mark was the first to offer to come out and help me to prepare the house and I was looking forward to his arrival a week before Sandra and Daisy were due. I soon realised however, that I should have warned him more explicitly about conditions. When we entered the little house where I had started, his reactions were stoical.

'Is this the best room in all these buildings?' he asked with a note of caution, almost panic. 'Are you going to put our new mattresses down on this rocky beach?' He emphasised the question by trying to scrape away loose boulders to reach a flat base. I knew he would be unsuccessful and tried a diversion by pointing out how the paint/*asvestis* combination was successfully holding back all stains on the walls.

We discussed priorities and agreed we should start by demolishing the low stonewall, about a metre high in the centre of the room, dividing the front area where people had lived from the rear part where I had removed the two rings for tethering animals. We could then at least create a level 'rocky beach.' This took the whole of the first day. We finished in the late afternoon and headed down for a swim, a shower and an early supper at the taverna.

On our first night at the house we flared up a gas lamp, which cast a warm yellow glow around the room, unknown to florescent lighting and electric bulbs. The cicadas had long since stopped clacking, olive trees rustled in the wind outside, one or two bats flitted through the sky. This first night was exciting. Nobody had slept in this little cluster of houses for more than thirty years. I was glad that Mark was there with me, taking everything in his stride and apparently not bothered by unfamiliar noises of the countryside.

In the cool of the early morning we awoke and were keen to get back to work. Early morning is the best time to carry building materials down from the top of the hill. At midday we would stop work for a picnic lunch with beer or wine and in the afternoon Mark would go wind surfing. Leaving the olive press at two in the afternoon, I could swim for half an hour and be back by three to do odd jobs around the house. In the evening, we would head to the taverna for an early supper, to avoid a walk back up the hillside after dark. It's not easy to negotiate the rocky parts of the path at night, even with a torch, under a Greek night sky of stars.

At the end of the first week the room was looking more domesticated. We carried water bags up from the taverna and had a wash bowl, a food safe, a gas cooker, a few books and some whisky. A number of agricultural and domestic implements were lying around the room, which we cleaned up and displayed along the top of the fireplace; a flat wooden palette with a long handle, used for lifting dough or bread from the baking oven; numerous pitchforks of hard wood, usually olive; a walking stick with a beautifully carved handle; single hooks, cut from branches, for moving brambles or releasing goats caught in brushwood. It was closer to camping than bourgeois comfort, but we were living where we wanted to be, in our own Greek house with one of the most beautiful views in the Mediterranean.

*

Mark was due to leave on the same plane that brought out Sandra and Daisy. I would miss him. After a week of working together we travelled to the airport with mixed feelings for our hellos and goodbyes. The airport at Zakynthos is well managed, but like others on small Greek Islands, restrictions were imposed due to surrounding mountains. In those days, the short runway meant that planes were often unable to take off, in the highest summer temperatures, with a full complement of passengers and sufficient fuel to reach London direct, and stops had to be scheduled for re-fuelling in Northern Italy. On one occasion an Italian airport official came aboard as we landed, to ask the pilot what we wanted and why we were there. It felt more like a stop to buy petrol; planes surely had radios for such purposes?

But seldom were there delays on the inward journey and Sandra and Daisy arrived, fresh from the damp grey skies of Gatwick, tired but on time. We saw Mark back off to England with thankyous and goodbyes; Daisy in particular was upset that she wouldn't be able to watch him windsurfing. But then it was time to head back to the north, for another first night at the house.

As we walked up the hill, I sensed my anxiety rising, but excitement too, about their first night at Margarita's olive press. There was still enough daylight so there were no problems about seeing where to climb. I walked ahead, leaving Daisy with Sandra to follow at a more leisurely rate. At the house I lit the gas lamps and found Daisy's furry leopard and put him on her pillow, then took a couple of lighted candles to the terrace, placing them on the stone seats by the doors of the olive press. Sandra and Daisy seemed a long time coming and I couldn't see them down the hillside. I got up and went to stand at the edge of the terrace, beginning to feel the slightest cool of anxiety. Suddenly Daisy was there with her arms tightly around my waist.

'Love the lights, Daddy, we could see them from down the hill...'

Sandra appeared on the terrace and put her arms around my neck; Daisy held firm; I put an arm round each – for an instant we were at the centre and the edge. Daisy unlocked her arms first and ran off down the steps, 'I want to see inside!'

I gave Sandra the iron key to the little house, rather ceremoniously.

'Key to your heart?' she asked.

'Perhaps. Lock the door first.'

Down in our room, Daisy was almost asleep, cuddling leopard. We kissed her goodnight and got into bed, turning the gas lights out and the reading lights on. They shone like glow-worms in the dark room.

Before we slept, I told them what a quiet peaceful place this was, you could sleep deeply until long after sunrise, but it needs getting used to for a couple of nights. From far below came the faint but regular thump of a diesel engine driving a boat out to sea for the night's fishing. Occasionally there was the higher pitch of a bird, probably an owl, the scratchings and scurryings of night 'squirrels,' fortunately not too close by. It was good not to hear cars. Later the wind picked up and branches of the great olive tree outside our door started brushing against the roof.

'Darling, can you hear the olive branches?'

'Yes,' she said.

'Tomorrow, I'll cut them back.'

'Yes,' she said.

We reached towards each other. All the waking ghosts tiptoed away to let us be and sleep.

Sometime in the middle of the night we were awoken by a great thump. Switching on a torch we saw that Daisy had fallen from her bed and lay motionless on the sharp boulders of the mountain. I jumped out and picked her up in my arms. Sandra examined her. There was no sign of harm. She was sleeping soundly.

At sunrise we were awoken by an appalling and momentarily frightening scream of aircraft engines immediately above us. An aircraft was roaring down the hillside, possibly in distress. We raced outside to see it passing overhead, almost shaking the olive trees as it passed, then descending to the *micro nisi*, where it levelled out over the sea. Suddenly another aircraft was above us, seemingly even lower. We expected machine-gun fire, cluster bombs even. Sandra mentioned paratroops, but they wouldn't have had any chance jumping at that height. These must be manoeuvres targeted on an empty ruined farmhouse, our olive press, mid-way down the hill. As the shock wore off we found a simpler explanation. It was not the military but the fire brigade. Flying level over the sea, the aircraft scoops seawater to fill up the body of the plane and rises again over the coast, to head off a forest fire somewhere inland. But here, thank God, no bombs, no fire. 'Breakfast would be a good idea,' said Sandra.

Soon we were all on the terrace drinking black coffee, eating peaches, yoghurt and honey, and feeling warmer in the morning sun. Daisy was sure she had slept, uninterrupted, throughout and hadn't even heard the aircraft at dawn. All things considered, it hadn't been such a bad first night.

*

After a week we were all beginning to feel that we were making the house our own. I went up to the village and bought groceries at Iannis' shop; he laughed at the story of aerial bombardment; I also mentioned that I planned to visit Margarita the following morning. When I arrived at her house I found her frying a large piece of oily fish, which was surely destined for me. Iannis had obviously told her I was coming to visit. I had already eaten breakfast, and fish at that time of the morning was definitely not appealing. Margarita said we should celebrate and, of course, I couldn't refuse. Fortunately, Dennis took the last helping of fish on my behalf. This was generously replaced by Margarita, with more platefuls, this time of a potent feta cheese. Eventually I finished the celebration breakfast and thanked her for taking such trouble.

'We've had a good summer at the olive press,' I said.

Margarita hesitated. 'You know the great olive grindstone?' she said. 'It's mine, you know. I haven't sold it.' After all the fish, I began to feel even more unwell.

'The great stone is built into the internal wall dividing the two rooms,' I said. 'It is part of the structure of the house, which I bought.'

'I haven't sold the stone,' she said.

'If you buy a house in England, or anywhere else, when the purchase is complete, everything in the house belongs to the new owner, unless it has been discussed and agreed beforehand.'

'I haven't sold the stone.'

'I'll talk to people in the village and see what they think about it.'

Margarita was hesitant again, but let the matter rest.

When I next saw her, early the following year, nothing was said about the grindstone. Instead she launched an attack to capture the *pithi*.

'The *pithi* which stands behind the double doors,' she was saying very firmly, 'we used it for the olive oil. I haven't sold it; it's mine.'

A year wiser, this time I tried a different method of defence.

'Margarita,' I said, 'you have been so kind to me, that when you finally sell us your last house there, at the end of the terrace, I would like to make you a gift of the *pithi*.'

She didn't reply but smiled, eyeing me carefully.

*

Later when I met Margarita again, we discussed buying her last property – the little two-story house attached to the olive press building, at the end of the terrace. Surprisingly, we reached agreement on price quite quickly and then made a plan that I would pick her up a week later, at the crossroads by her house in the village.

On the agreed day, I travelled with Panaiotis, an engineer, whom I had asked to draw up the necessary plan of the building and associated land. It was a big mistake to accept his offer to drive. He handled his car like a frustrated racing driver, irked by hairpin bends, disregarding speed and other drivers on both sides of the road. After collecting Margarita we arrived frightened and exhausted at the bottom of our hill and divided the survey equipment between the three of us. Margarita chose the heaviest item and only agreed to exchange it for something lighter as we finally approached the olive press. Panaiotis began his survey and Margarita entered her upper room, unused for more than twenty years, and started to remove some of her last few possessions. Into a large plastic bag she put a mirror, an oil lamp, a rusted chopper for firewood and the flaking gilt frame and icon of the Virgin Mary. She left behind discarded clothing, old shoes and a few plastic sheets and piles of straw.

Margarita was frowning as she came out of the room and began to mutter about a higher price. Rather as thunder and darkening skies approach from the horizon with gathering strength, so Margarita began a campaign, which unlike a storm, was clearly not intended to blow over.

Panaiotis joined us and said he could not continue if there was disagreement. I said we had already reached agreement and there was no reason to change it. Margarita insisted that the new price she was now asking was a fair one. On past evidence, I decided that any agreement to a higher price now would only provoke more brinkmanship later at the office of the *symvoleographos*. Margarita walked with me down to the lower terrace discussing the matter with her usual vigour, away from Panaiotis and away from the problem of losing face if she changed her mind. But losing face was not one of her concerns, I decided, and she stuck to her new position. Nothing could now be done but pack up and walk back down the hill. Panaiotis was angry; I expressed the hope that we would all be alive twelve months hence to discuss it all again; Margarita was very cross to have lost the deal.

At that point I also had a more immediate concern, which was how our grand prix driver would make up for so much lost time on the return journey. The best approach, I decided, was to keep Panaiotis talking. As we drove back to the village, even Margarita was worried and relieved eventually to get out of the car. But Panaiotis couldn't maintain his racetrack speeds when, at every sharp bend, he had a new question to answer. Incentives are always helpful in language learning and my fluency in Greek improved dramatically. But the nervous system took days to recover.

The following summer Margarita and I went back to the olive press together. As we were walking round her eye fell upon the *pithi*. We looked at each other.

She said, 'I give you the *pithi*.'

The deal was concluded. Sterling/Drachmas exchange rates had moved significantly in favour of sterling and Greek inflation that year had not been particularly high, so we could now happily agree Margarita's higher price, which ditched the previous deal. But I already knew it wasn't really a question of price. Into her plastic bag she had put a few remaining memories of half a lifetime there and couldn't let go. At the office of the *symvoleographos* everything went according to plan and Lambis supervised the swift emergence of the contract with agreement from all concerned. For once Margarita was in no mood for brinkmanship. The time for her to say goodbye to her Olive Press had come and we were ready to take the helm.

7

Master Builder
Choose a middle aged house without the building faults of youth
or the failings of old age

My time at the olive press has taught me many tricks about the restoration of an old Greek house. In the restoration of the buildings the challenges have sometimes seemed insurmountable, but the effort is always rewarded. And if you are interested in history, buildings or DIY, you will understand why the project was irresistible. *Prepare la casa* had begun and Dionysius' observation stayed with me. Of course we learnt as we went along, since there are no textbooks on ways to restore a small hamlet of ancient stone houses, half way up a Greek mountain, with no road. Even builders interested in such a project were few and far between, so finding one who was both skilled and willing, would be the first step.

I had heard from my friend Nionio that there was a builder, Andreas, who lived in the village and was well respected locally. He arranged for Andreas to visit the olive press one morning, though after my first experience with local builders my anticipation was cautious. His son, Giorgos, appeared to find the steep walk rather an effort. But I was relieved that they did not appear to be too surprised by what they found when they came and was pleased when Andreas gave me directions to his house in the village, so I could visit them to finalise plans and costs.

After a few days, I arrived at their house as arranged, a little late but not by the standards of rural 'Greek time'. Andreas was nowhere to be seen, but his friendly wife told me that he was working in another village and invited me in for a coffee. Giorgos was resting. Soon he appeared sleepily in the doorway and I asked him why his father was not here to discuss the job. He replied quite simply.

'Too difficult.'

'Where's he working?'

'Not far, in another village.'

'Show me where,' I said. 'I'll drive you.' Giorgos seemed keen at the prospect of travelling in some comfortable foreign car, and agreed to come. When he saw my dusty moped he reacted with undisguised disdain and made a vigorous attempt to get out of the whole affair. But soon we were bumping up and down on rough roads, travelling northwards, high over scrub and heath-land, past long lines of grey stone walls and tall cypresses that grew in sheltered folds and valleys. The sea lay to the left and could also be seen through gaps in the hills on the right. After about four miles Giorgos indicated a little stone house with grey roof tiles.

'He's there somewhere.'

Andreas was inside the first room, plastering the ceiling. He showed no surprise at seeing us and carried on plastering as I spoke. After a while he stopped.

'Your house is too much work,' he said. 'Walls, roofs, floors, windows, doors... Maybe if there was a road... but there's not even a way to get sand and cement and the other things necessary to build a house there. It's impossible, I cannot do it.'

He was beginning to sound like the other builders. If I don't land him now, I thought, we would have to go through this all again with somebody else. I decided to launch the main argument.

'Mules,' I said.

'Mules?' he looked as if he had never heard of the animals. Young Giorgos, whose main job was in the merchant navy and who had visited many of the world's great ports and cities – Rotterdam, London, Hong Kong – now looked on with contempt. First a moped, now mules, where would this end?

'Yes, mules!' I said. 'All the most famous buildings of ancient Greece were built with mules – the Parthenon was built with mules – and you say you can't even put a bit of cement on my house, down the hillside?'

Andreas paused.

'I'll do it,' he said, and quoted a modest sum of drachmas. Then he added, 'You organise the mules.'

Game, set and match to Andreas. He knew as well as I did that finding a mule, even in those days, would be a major problem. But like the best of Napoleon's generals, luck was still on my side and I remembered seeing a mule at the top of the hill near Iannis' house. So Giorgos and I got back on the moped and travelled off to find him. When we reached the end of the familiar track we discovered Iannis sitting peacefully on his shaded terrace. He gave us good news. At least, half of it was good. He had a mule that he was prepared to take up and down the track with building materials. The price was the bad half.

'Mine is the only mule in many kilometres from here,' he said. He was exaggerating I thought, to emphasise a monopoly position.

'I could hire a car at that rate,' I said.

'A car can't get down to your house carrying cement or anything else.'

Any other mule would be located further away, so even at a lower rate, the final price might easily be higher. It could also be useful to have a friendly Iannis with his mule, at the top of the hill. I agreed his daily rate. Discussion with Giorgos determined the quantities of sand and cement required and Iannis said his mule would take three days. He needed payment in advance.

Andreas and Giorgio started work surprisingly quickly, while Iannis walked his mule down the rocky track from the top, loaded first with cement bags and later with white sand in open sacks. He piled the sand high on our lovely terrace, which he could see made me distinctly unhappy.

'Where else can I put it?' he asked.

The first job was to mix up the cement. Since there was no water in our *sterna*, we looked for others in the area and found three. The rear roof of the little house acted as a water collector, shooting rain down into the overgrown opening of one small *sterna*, and there were two others located in fields further down the hill. All contained water, which we were glad not to have to drink, though with rough filtering it was adequate for the cement. We carried the water in buckets and stored it in the *pithi* – perhaps the first time in more than fifty years that it was being used, albeit for humble water rather than precious olive oil. In times of need both are precious, but forced by choice, even olive oil gives place to water.

When a place is very beautiful it is easy to forget that certain basics must be secured in order for it to also be habitable. The first of these is the water supply. Our primary concern was therefore to reinforce the cylindrical wall of the enormous *sterna* in the olive press. To enter the *sterna*, Andreas had to move the heavy stone through which buckets were dropped to draw up water. He lowered our longest ladder, used for the olive harvest, and began to clean all the surfaces. The bottom was thick with broken pieces of rock, dried leaves, shrivelled olives and the bones of small animals and snakes, which had fallen and drowned in their search for water. Giorgos pulled up buckets of gunge and sharp hard objects until finally the floor and sides of the *sterna* were clear and clean enough to take cement.

When I next looked down with a torch, two days later, I could see what an excellent job had been done. Andreas was proud of it and was smiling. Giorgos had lost his disdain and was sharing the credit.

'That will hold much beautiful water for you,' said Andreas and I thanked him for a job really well done in difficult circumstances. We walked down the terrace to the little house discussing the proposed cement floor that was needed there. The floor that Daisy had fallen onto was pure mountain rock, formed out of rough and uneven boulders. There were also a few boulders in the corners of the room that could not be covered without raising the whole floor to an unacceptable height, so we agreed to keep that corner of the mountain in the room. Andreas promised the job would be done and ready for next summer. But before we returned next summer, a catastrophe would strike at the olive press building and problems of much greater importance than the laying of a cement floor would require our attention.

*

We heard the news on a bitterly cold February day in London, when thoughts of Margarita's olive press and the surrounding Ionian were of mildness and wellbeing.

'It's bad news.' Lambis was on the phone.

What was he talking about?

'It's very bad, I'm afraid. The roof's gone.'

'Roof? What roof?' I asked.

'It's the roof of the olive press building. There's been a snowfall. The heaviest since 1926, according to the newspaper. It's particularly bad at the northern end of the island, where many people are cut off. Nionio phoned me from the *psari* taverna. He said everybody heard your roof crashing to the ground like an explosion in a quarry. They even heard it at the top of the hill. He went up to look at the damage before ringing me. It's very bad; two thirds of the roof has completely collapsed. Cross-timbers, rafters, boards, tiles – everything is on the ground. It's like the after-effects of an earthquake or a bombardment up there.'

I interrupted to ask if there was damage to the fireplace or *sterna* top, and what about the *pithi*?

'Nionio didn't mention any of those things; it's most unlikely that they escaped damage.'

'Did he say if the little house was all right?'

'Yes, it seems to be unaffected. Of course it has a much smaller roof.'

'And in much better condition,' I said, looking for something positive amid the devastation.

'You can stay there while you rebuild the main roof,' said Lambis a little more cheerfully. The prospect of rebuilding the entire timber structure of the roof, over a nine-metre span halfway up the mountainside, was the most daunting I had faced so far.

None of our friends really believed the possibility of two metres of snow on a Greek island bringing down a roof. Surely a light snowfall and a few dislodged tiles were more realistic? But no, our Greek house no longer had a roof. We had never before owned a house without a roof. You could have a house without a proper floor, or a wall or two, but not without a roof. A building without a roof was either a ruin or a building site; it was certainly not a house.

'Let's take the next flight out to see the disaster for ourselves,' was the natural reaction; but what further damage could happen? Did we really need to go now? We decided first to ask Andreas for a quote to rebuild the roof and to check whether any immediate work would be required for safety or to prevent further damage. He replied within a month, but his quotation was extremely high, due mainly to transport costs. Another builder would be unlikely to quote significantly less and because of the difficulties might not even be interested. The only other alternative was to consider rebuilding the roof ourselves. This was a fine thought, and for a moment the challenge of the thought obscured the reality; and as the questions multiplied, the project, surprisingly, seemed more feasible rather than less. We would bring out a couple of students who were practical and keen on DIY; Lambis or Nionio would tell us where to buy tools and building materials; Lambis would probably know an architect or engineer whom we could engage to specify the appropriate structure, something which might be safe against earthquakes. The transport problem was really a simple choice; either we carried materials down manually or we hired Iannis and his mule. Nothing else was needed except hard work, organisation and persistence. Good luck and drachmas would help too.

According to my stepson Dominic I was trying to 'recapture my youth.' I replied that surely there were better ways of doing that. 'You are not a young man any longer, Rodney,' he would say. I remembered a scene, ten years before, when a client of mine, a rich Saudi Sheikh, had a vigorous argument with me and I deliberately gave him the impression I was very angry. The following day he seemed relieved to find I had not left Riyadh on the first available plane. He was speaking to his principal aide, a fluent and clever Egyptian called Mahmoud, who then turned to me and said, 'The Sheikh says that you should not have got angry with him yesterday, since you are an old man.'

In fact I was in my early forties. I didn't react. There was a pause. Mahmoud turned to the Sheikh, a clutter of Arabic firing out like a faulty Kalashnikov. Then Mahmoud turned to me.

'The Sheikh says that you should not have got angry with him yesterday, since you are no longer a young man.'

It was a fine distinction and nicely phrased, just like Dominic ten years later. For how much longer can such subtleties be sustained? I could hear Mahmoud saying, 'The Sheikh says you should not attempt to build a roof like that since you are now...' and then he would hesitate, not wishing to repeat a discourtesy, but uncertain now of the category which could combine courtesy with reality, 'an older man.' That's okay.

The first volunteer for the building team was Sandra's nephew Jonathan. He was practical with tools and worked in Cambridge building greenhouses, not exactly comparable but good experience, I felt sure. The next candidate was Thomas, a tall strong German. He was a friend of Lucy's who had worked on building sites in England and Germany. The third member of the team was my nephew Nick, who was also very practical. His particular experience of welding could be useful if we wanted to build a special wheelbarrow for the mule track.

In July, we each came to the island according to schedule, except for Thomas who arrived ten days early and found his way to the *micro nisi* and the *psari* taverna. He stayed there to wait for us, quickly making good friends with Nionio and was given lodging and very full board in return for odd jobs around the taverna and fishing trips with Nionio every morning. He swam in the afternoons and enjoyed a pleasing life of luxury and interest. For somebody less scrupulous in keeping arrangements than Thomas, this could have been very unfortunate. He was understandably reluctant to exchange all this for work on the mountain building site. But he kept to our arrangement.

*

On the high ground above the olive press I stood looking down on the remains of the devastated roof. There were huge cavities where fallen beams had been embedded at the top of the walls. Many stone blocks had been thrown to the floor as the timbers fell. They lay amid deep piles of splintered rafters and shattered tiles. This roof should have lasted another thirty years. Fortunately the *sterna, pithi,* fireplace and grindstone, the four most precious items in the room, were unharmed. I looked up to see, above, wild waving olive branches and below the calm blue sea. A lovely spot for a building site. Pity about the access!

Good technical advice would be vital. Lambis introduced me to Spiros, the engineer who had done the *skedio* for the purchase contract. My thanks to Spiros for coming would have been even greater had I known that he was not going to make any charge for the visit. He spoke little

English but was fluent in Italian, having been a student of architecture in Rome. Unfortunately my conversation became a complete muddle; I wasn't competent yet in Greek and my Italian fell to pieces, with Greek emerging in place of Italian words I had known for thirty years.

We all agreed the roof was a mess.

'You'll be much better off under a nice new roof,' said Lambis.

'These old timbers couldn't have lasted much longer anyway,' said Spiros. 'Look at the woodworm. You were lucky not to be here when it happened.'

A small part of the roof was still standing.

'You should rebuild that too as soon as possible,' Spiros commented.

'In case of another snowfall?' I asked.

Spiros wasn't amused. 'You need a new timber structure like the one I built for the theatre in Zakynthos town. Cover it with corrugated cement sheeting and put back a single layer of old tiles on top. It will look identical to the original roof outside and inside you can clad it with wooden boards. You should cement the ridge tiles to keep them safe against the winter gales.'

He drew a rough sketch showing timber lengths and angles and continued;

'You will need to make sure that all of your beams are level. This is very simple if you use the Roman method. I will tell you how. Take a long, small, flexible pipe, made of leather if you want to be Roman, or plastic if you want to be practical, and fill it with water. Lay the pipe across the floor of the room and take each end up to the top of the walls, where the ends of the cross beam are to rest. Water, of course, finds its own level, so you can immediately judge whether the beam-ends are of equal height, by the water level in the pipe. It's much better than trying to use a spirit level on uneven timbers over a wide span.

'There is one more thing I must tell you. This is very important in earthquake areas. To support the roof in the right way, you must build wooden "diamond patterns" in the centre of the roof, under the apex of each "A" frame. It's the latest design and gives maximum protection against earthquake stresses. The rafters and sheeting give the necessary lateral stability so don't leave the frames for long without fixing some battens across them. That's really all you need to know. Good luck.'

Many, many years later, in the Oratorio di San Giovanni Battista in Urbino, built in the 14th century, I looked up at the wooden vaulted ceiling and could see, above each of the cross beams, Spiros' diamond pattern. Six hundred years old. Good enough for our structure then.

*

We spent a week clearing the wreckage. Rotten wood was burnt in small quantities, to prevent sparks rising up over the walls into the dry countryside. Nobody wanted a visit by planes from the fire brigade, bombing the new roof with hundreds of gallons of sea-water.

When I next saw Lambis he took me to a marvellous old-fashioned hardware shop in the old part of Zakynthos town. Walls were stacked with boxes from floor to ceiling, bursting with ironmongery for every possible use and application. Wires, pipes, tubes, string, and grills hung from straps and hooks in the ceiling. Hi-tech equipment was displayed or scattered over the counter or the floor. I was able to buy all the tools, nails, screws and bolts on my shopping list.

The next step was to organise transport for timber and roofing sheets. 'We have a good system here,' said Lambis. 'There is a street on the other side of town which is used as a lorry rank. It works like a taxi rank. I know one of the drivers, Dino. He's reliable and quotes reasonable prices. We'll try him first.' We found him sitting in the shade chatting with a group of drivers, all of whom were waiting for their next assignment. We discussed the load of cement sheets and timber to be collected at the builders' merchants. He roughly knew the location of the little village at the top of our hill but we agreed to travel together.

Travelling back to the olive press, we were a curious couple. The ageing open-bed lorry was heavily laden with cement sheets. Enormous lengths of timber were piled high over the roof of the cab and projected far forward, like multiples of Don Quixote's lance. Dino's round bronze face peered out anxiously at the risky bends and crossroads along the way. If he was Don Quixote, I must have been Sancho Panza, astride the saddle of a bright red moped, grey hair blowing untidily in the wind, certainly no longer a young man, but in the lead, none the less. Together we drove up through the grande corniche from the coast to the northern plateau; we scaled the steep climb through the village and up through the church square; we reached the top of the ridge, threw caution to the winds and sailed down the whole length of the eastern slopes of the mountain, in the style of Spanish galleons. Everyone saw us passing through the village and were keen to joke about it when they saw me next.

We arrived at the top of our hill without mishap and I helped Dino to unload. Although Giorgos had given us permission, I was embarrassed to see the vast pile of building materials which spread over their garden, but they were friendly and helpful and Dino assured me that they didn't mind. A few years later when we were due to receive another large delivery of building materials in Giorgos' garden we brought, from England, a present for him and his wife – a cut glass dish, with sections for olives and nuts, mounted in a silver plated holder. Was it appropriate? I wasn't sure but they appeared to like it and if they didn't, they could always sell it.

Dino left saying he would collect the agreed drachmas from Lambis. The whole operation had gone surprisingly smoothly. From start to finish in eight hours we had gathered everything needed to build a roof. No delivery problems, nothing 'partially complete', no queues or delays, no need for forward ordering, no computer invoices to follow. Could this have been done in London or Frankfurt? I preferred the Greek way. But carrying it all down to the Olive Press was another matter.

The following morning we tried to bring down the cement sheets. After great expense of energy and time we managed to carry just two sheets down to the olive press. The task was almost impossible. The sheets just could not be handled in the space available on the mule track, the weight was crippling and the length made it difficult, in certain steep places, to lift them high enough to clear the larger rocks. I managed to telephone the builders' merchant from the taverna and discovered that they had shorter sheets that they were prepared to exchange. I spoke to Lambis who then contacted Dino. The following day, all the concrete sheets at the top of the hill were exchanged for shorter ones. Get it right in the first place and you may still be on the nursery slopes; putting right what has gone wrong is the real test. Who was I kidding? It was a time consuming and expensive mistake.

Two people could carry the shorter sheets, two at a time, held at each end by ropes, slung beneath a long length of cypress tree trunk. We had earlier made a sling from two lengths of rafters, which Thomas had left behind on a wall at the top of the hill, from where it had disappeared. Frustrated, I turned to him. 'Do you remember Schiller's famous quotation, Thomas? "Against stupidity, even the Gods fight in vain."' It may have upset him and I immediately regretted it. Nothing, certainly not the sling, was worth upsetting my helper and friend. Fortunately Thomas was robust and didn't immediately quit the site for the good life down at the taverna.

The system for bringing down the sheets worked quite well, but the real problem now was the big timbers. A foot square and almost thirty feet long, each piece had to be carried by only two people. If a third tried to help, in the middle, he was crushed like an inefficient fulcrum under a seesaw. If others tried to help at the ends, they got in the way on the narrow path. I carried down the front end of the beam, to crush any attempts at recapturing my youth. The remaining four beams were brought down by Jonathan and Thomas, each morning for the rest of the week. Only Thomas was strong enough to carry a full cement bag the whole way down.

One morning when Thomas and Jonathan had carried down a particularly heavy piece of timber, Thomas was angry and depressed.

'They're just laughing at us up there. I am sure they think we are nothing but mules, doing this work!'

'No, I am sure not,' I said. 'Giorgos was once a strong man himself. Now he is old and feeble; he can't walk without a stick. Every time you pick up those timbers, you remind him of his youth when he could also do such things. Now he is full of regret, not laughter.'

Thomas looked doubtful; Jonathan shrugged; the job had to be done.

'*Mulari angli* – English Mules,' I said later to our friends at the top. Like many country folk anywhere in the world, they were not always the best of friends with their neighbour Iannis, who owned the mule which we had used for transporting the first loads of sand and cement. I think they may not have been sorry to see Iannis and his mule denied the lucrative work which we English mules were now undertaking instead.

*

July is the hottest month on the island and an enclosed rock structure without shade, like the olive press building, is not a good place to work. By the time we stopped for lunch at midday, the room would be a white-hot oven. Every morning Thomas brought up, from the taverna, our lunchtime picnic made by Nionio's wife, Diamanto, who always included choriatiki salad, extra feta cheese, boiled eggs and plentiful slices of heavy brown bread. Sometimes she would add bottles of beer, which we would make a priority to keep cool. The picnic came in a big white plastic box, so these feasts became known as 'picnic plastico.'

Thomas was reaching the end of his two-week commitment and was talking about returning to Germany. There was one job for which I particularly needed his muscular help and the following morning he and I deserted our fellow roof-builder Jonathan to start the most unpleasant task we had yet undertaken. This was the removal of all the straw from the inner room of the little house. I had already tried to interest Nionio and his friends in taking it, but nobody had a use for it and all my offers were met with polite disinterest. Our first problem was what to do with it. It would be too dangerous to burn during the summer months. We could think of no practical use for it and finally decided to spread it over the garden area at the end of the house where hopefully it would rot away over the next couple of winters. We planned to use two plastic ground sheets. Thomas would use one to carry the straw from the room to the edge of the terrace and tip it over to the lower terrace. I would gather it into the other tarpaulin and carry it to the garden.

'Be very careful of snakes, Thomas', I warned. 'They like straw and could be nesting anywhere.'

Once we started working, I soon discovered that I could hardly keep up with Thomas, despite working at my fastest. Gradually the stockpile on the lower terrace increased and began to spread over the surrounding rocks. We both wore plastic bags on our heads but the dust from the straw got in everywhere, causing unbearable irritation to the skin. We stopped, or rather crumpled after about two hours, in agreement that even working with stone and wood in the open furnace of the open olive press building was preferable to humping straw around. When we resumed our task, Thomas took the outside job and I went into the inner room. Thomas was striding back and forth to the garden and soon cleared the backlog of straw that I had accumulated. No stockpile of straw was building up on the lower terrace. I realised that years of experience as a management consultant in productivity improvement must now be put to the test. In fact the solution was simple. Sitting on top of the baking oven were some ancient wooden pitch-forks, selected and cut from branches for their antler like qualities. I chose one and set to work shifting straw at about twice the rate that I had managed by hand. Gradually the stockpile of straw on the lower terrace increased, in direct proportion to Thomas' surprise and irritation at the mysterious increase in pace. Eventually I cleared the room entirely. Thomas laughed when I showed him what had been happening and said, 'You should have thought of it when we started. We'd have finished long ago. By the way,' he continued, 'I've never worked so hard on a building site; never in Germany, never in Israel, never in England.' What more could I say than, 'Thank you. We couldn't have done it without you.'

By the time Thomas left, we had placed all five cross beams in position and built up the stone-work where they met the walls at each end. It was a good level base from which to build the rest of the wooden structure. Jonathan stayed another ten days and made a fine contribution in carpentry, stone work and general hard labour down the mule track. Sandra and Daisy were now due to arrive with my nephew, Nick. As planned, early one morning before sunrise, I drove to the airport and saw a huddled group of three waiting on the pavement outside the main building. There had been a misunderstanding; the flight had landed more than two hours before.

I now wondered if there had been other misunderstandings. Nick arrived with two fine leather suitcases and a smart Harris tweed jacket. He was fond of Greece and had even worked for a while as a welder at Nauplion, in the Peloponnese. I had carefully described our location to him but his earlier experiences of cosmopolitan life in the tavernas and bars of the port of Nauplion had somehow been transported to the shore-line opposite the *micro nisi*. Had he imagined the taverna come to life, night after night, with bazouki music and dance, the tinkle of ouzo glasses and the laughter of Greek girls with eyes shaped like Kalamata olives? Instead there is the *psari* taverna where Diamanto shuffles forward with nothing but the moon or the sun and the sound of the waves for miles around.

Nick didn't much appreciate the remote position and the primitive conditions of the olive press. The night there didn't suit him; I could understand why. However, the first few days of his visit were spent in town. With the help of Lambis we had located a workshop, which had welding equipment and where Nick would be able to work. The plan was to design and build a form of wheel-barrow, which could be used to carry materials down the mule track. He spent three days building a marvellous machine that we called the Nickmobile. It was good for carrying cement and other sacks, but stability was a problem and the only wheel we could find for it was rather too small.

Exactly seven weeks from the day we started, I fixed the last cement sheet in position and covered the top of the end wall with tiles. Everything would be dry during the winter and even more important, rainwater could now flow down the newly fixed guttering into the *sterna*. Next summer, three years after buying Margarita's olive press, we would have water. Never buy a place without water?

*

In the following May, Mark and I flew out together to work on the roof of the little house. The main wooden structure was sound but most of the boards supporting the tiles had been turned to powder by generations of woodworm. The job of carrying cement sheets down the mule track was as hard as it had been for the big roof and as before we did it at sunrise. During the afternoons, Mark would go windsurfing. From time to time I enjoyed looking out at the sea trying to spot the fastest sail in the east. The only one, as it happened. The following morning at dawn we would be back at work. The whole operation took just two weeks.

Another year, we tackled the remaining one third of the great roof over the olive press building, which had somehow survived the winter of the heavy snow. Unlike the chaos of the first year, we were able to take down the tiles and timbers in an orderly manner to minimise damage to the tops of the walls. Mark and I were helped by a friend of his from London, another Sam, who travelled out with me in the camping-van, via Yugoslavia. Soon after entering Greece we passed a turning to Delphi and since Sam had never been there, we turned off for a few hours. Surely the great oracle would not have been amused if travellers, passing so close, had failed to make a detour and pay their respects? What subsequent tribute might have been exacted in recompense for such discourtesy? Another roof might need to be sacrificed.

In fact, 'Another year, another roof,' was becoming the motto. This time we restored the roof of the second house we had bought from Margarita, the middle house. Everything went according to plan, but we ran out of time for the final job: cementing of the ridge tiles. I asked Andreas. 'I will do it before the start of the winter rains,' he promised. Then, 'Have you got time to pick cherries? Come on Sunday.'

Early Sunday morning, I met Andreas at his house in Upper Volimes, high above the church, with a view across a little cemetery and the wide plateau. Andreas had done what many builders do in their spare time and turned his house into a particular palace of his own, with terraces and tiles, patios and vines, prospects and shadows. No doubt about the quality of the workmanship. As we climbed onto his tractor, he told me he was building a house for himself in the hills outside the village and years before had planted a cherry orchard. He was popular with the birds, at this time of the year, when the cherries were ripe for eating.

Andreas drove his tractor and trailer down the steep road around the church and through the square. It was a bright morning and drifts of cool air from the night before could still be sensed. Shadows lay pale and long; dogs were sleeping; their owners stirring; the shop and the taverna were open. I had seldom seen them shut. At the bottom of the square, Andreas turned into a narrow lane beside the taverna. One or two people waved as we passed. Then as we turned a bend in the lane, we found ourselves facing another tractor, towing a great wagon of hay. Both tractors stopped and tactics were reviewed by the two drivers. A moment later, the other tractor advanced decisively a few yards and stopped again. Then negotiations burst out and continued for more than ten minutes. I wondered what possible compromise could allow us free passage to the cherry orchard before midday. Suddenly it seemed agreement had been reached, much to the disappointment of ten or twelve onlookers who may have hoped for longer diversion. Among them was Marinos who agreed that a democratic solution was inappropriate.

Andreas motioned me down from the tractor as he got down himself. To my surprise, the other driver walked over and climbed into Andreas' cab, took off the brake and tried to engage the reverse gear, with much grinding and failure. Frustration growing and in anger, he practically wrenched the gear lever out of its mounting. Andreas judged it nicely as he balanced his own tractor's gear rupture against barely apparent 'Schadenfreude'. He told me later that the gear was faulty and difficult to engage. Indeed, I thought. Eventually, he showed the other driver how to engage the gear and let him reverse the tractor and trailer down the narrow lane. A trailer is never easily reversed, but for the unfamiliar, with a gear on the verge of breakdown and a narrow lane lined on both sides with spectators, including children, the result could be close to chaos. Finally tractor and trailer backed their way into the square, without casualty to anything or anybody apart from the driver himself, who had given twenty minutes of entertainment and suffered a sharp dent in his reputation, despite the worthiest of efforts. The art of successful retreat is a foremost political skill and I was reminded to keep clear of political encounters with Andreas.

At the taverna, we picked up a couple of bottles of lemonade and renewed our journey. Soon we were driving on a dirt road among bare brown hills on one side and a green valley of olives and cypress on the other. We passed a few low stone farmhouses with goats and chickens; skinny brown and black dogs yapped their way towards us, half-heartedly, before slinking back to their chosen patch of shade, wagging their tails apologetically. After half an hour, Andreas suddenly swung the tractor from the road and stopped. We walked down a bank and crossed a dry riverbed to reach his cherry orchard. The orchard was lush with trees – many olives, a few pear trees and well-spaced cherries. In the distance I could see his new house, built with breezeblocks, and very pleasant unless like me you prefer old houses. But I was certainly not going to argue with Andreas, who might easily manoeuvre me into an unsustainable position and costly retreat!

Andreas gave me some plastic bags and a long ladder and went off to work on his house. It was a lovely way to spend a sunny Sunday morning, up in the treetops surrounded by the song of little grey birds and the hum of bees. The cherries were dark and ripe and they dripped from the branches in abundance. I gathered up some bags to take back to Sandra. When Andreas called out that he wanted to return, we put away the ladder and got back onto his tractor. Surprisingly perhaps we managed to drive the whole way back to his house without incident.

*

So far our building agenda has given more priority to roofs than to floors. The floor of the olive press building still needs to be completely cleared of accumulated rubble, rocks and debris from the winter when the roof fell in. We haven't yet determined the state of the present floor, whether it is paved or just the basic rock of the hillside. In the middle house however, it was clear that the floor needed urgent attention; most of the boards had rotted dangerously and although we had patched it temporarily two years earlier, all needed replacing. My son Sam and his future wife Karen came out for a couple of weeks to help with the job.

By the entrance door we decided to build a staircase down to the lower room. We checked the old cypress floor joists and found all but one to be in good condition. The lower room had been used for animals and a wide shallow trough had been chiselled out of the stone floor for their drinking water. If the trough had been any deeper, we could have used it as a bath! The low ceiling joists made it unlikely that people had ever used the room, so to give reasonable headroom, every joist had to be raised by about eight inches. We engaged the indomitable Dino for the transportation of tongued and grooved floorboards, temporarily financed as usual by Lambis. Our biggest difficulties involved moving the old joists up to their new positions. The walls were half a metre thick and the joists projected deeply into them; they were secured with what must have been the largest available rocks. The floor joists had been placed into the walls as they were built and the rocks which held them in place were therefore integral to the whole structure of the house.

Eventually we completed the job, focusing on the movement of joists and the rebuilding of gaping holes left in the walls. Fitting the floor itself took less than a day. The new floor height allowed a better view of the sea; the wide stone window ledge could now be used as a window seat and the high sloping roof continued to give a spacious feel to the room.

During all this Sam and Karen had been dreaming some plans of their own. They had followed the footpath from the lower terrace, past our little hamlet and down to a large semi-circular field surrounded by steep mountain on all sides. It is a strange peaceful area and beautifully terraced, with a garden valley of cypress trees immediately in front of it. There are three more *sterna* there and a stone washing basin, indicating that more than one family once lived there. Sam's interest was aroused by a ruined house with collapsed stone walls and no sign of a roof. 'It would be wonderful to be able to restore something as far gone as this,' he said. 'Do you know who owns it?'

*

Building work at the olive press stretches out for years ahead; doors, windows, plumbing, wiring, everything but roofs. When I consider the work ahead I usually decide that building a road, up from below, is the only practical solution. But there are many reasons here to forget the practical; the wildness, the view, the challenge itself perhaps. Over the years many builders and helpers have come and gone, each leaving their own mark. In the stone of newly strengthened walls or the cypress beams of a new roof, everyone who has helped to breathe new life into the olive press becomes part of its history, and is remembered.

8

Ways and Means
Time expands for purpose. Extend the present moment

At the olive press nothing is quite as simple as turning on a switch or a tap and then paying the quarterly bills. Here we have no bills other than what we spend in the shop or the taverna. The luxuries of speed and convenience, which have their advantages, are replaced by new freedoms. Some systems have to be developed to make life here possible, others are more mundane. Part of how we make this wild place home for a summer every year is learning how to deal with snakes and doing the washing and cooking and purifying water and, and, and...

The first thing to check when I return is the water level in the *sterna*. With a torch and pitchfork I open wide the double doors of the olive press building. Light floods in, racing to the far corners of this great chamber. Then I slowly and carefully raise the wooden lid of the *sterna*. This wariness is not a precaution against water spirits taking flight, but against snakes. For it has been impossible to locate and block the secret passages of snakes. Dark poisonous little vipers or big slow grass snakes often find a way in, probably through holes high up in the hillside rock at the back of the *sterna*. Some people deliberately leave a stick trailing in the water to allow snakes to climb out. This may be acceptable where the *sterna* is away from the house, but I am reluctant to attract snakes to drink at my water-hole inside the house, whatever the cost of missing, as D.H. Lawrence put it, 'my chance with one of the lords of life'.

When snakes drown they float for a while on the surface of the water, turn white, then sink. One year an empty plastic water bottle fell unnoticed into the *sterna* and was found the following year, with a long grass snake coiled around its length like a boa constrictor, fighting to preserve its life. I wondered what it had found to eat during its time in the pitch black of the *sterna*. But my problem, whether they are dead or alive, is how to get them out.

Anything which falls into the *sterna* is difficult to retrieve. Before we had a fridge, we used to keep cheese, fruit, vegetables, and wine in the *sterna*, as many local people still do. The coolest practical place is just above the water level. We would fill baskets with everything we wanted to keep cool and lower them on ropes to the water level. Apart from missing the ease of simply opening a fridge door when you want, you find the only disadvantage of the *sterna* fridge is the difficulty of raising a water bucket through the access hole at the top, when half the contents of a supermarket cool counter is swinging on ropes below.

Sooner or later, it was inevitable that produce would be knocked from the swing into the deep water below. I was in town buying nails and wood when it happened. Sandra had flicked the edge of a shallow basket with the bucket when she was drawing water. Feta and doppio cheeses, some butter and a large carton of yoghurt fell in. These bobbed about fortunately without sinking, so when I returned an hour later I found Sandra and Daisy bending through the top of the *sterna*, fishing with a plastic bucket and failing to rescue a single item. Anything that disturbed the surface of the water caused the item to float away in the opposite direction. A basket of wire netting with a wide open top was the solution. Lowered under the targeted piece of cheese and lifted up slowly, the net lets the water pass through its mesh without disturbance and the cheese is easily recaptured. It took about five minutes. I was rightly chastised for self-satisfaction.

The same method is used for snakes. The dead ones which are still floating are the easiest; those at the bottom are fished out with the very long mast of Mark's windsurf board; but the live ones need more care. Those that are definitely grass snakes can be lifted out on the wire basket and carried as far towards the door as their weavings and wrigglings will allow; with luck, they'll slither away down the terrace to the safety of undergrowth and rocks. With vipers and others that may be poisonous, I hold a heavy stick and know exactly where I plan to put the basket. Risks are not to be taken with frightened or angry snakes. I try to lift the snake out quickly amid hissing, lips curling and open fangs, put it down and hit it on the head. The last time this happened I asked Daisy to stay in the little house until it was over. It took longer than usual and she imagined a mistake, a slip, a break in the cord; I might be lying on the floor as a snake, or more than one, passes over to sink through dark holes among the rocks. Bravely she came to find me and cried to find me alive and well.

Water in the *sterna* is our most precious commodity here. It enters as pure rainwater, mainly during the winter and early spring and is stored ready for our return the following summer. To make it quite safe for drinking purposes, I add a purification tablet to a five-litre water bottle and let it stand for an hour. The tablets are made in Switzerland and leave not a trace of flavour, unlike chlorine tablets that make you feel that you could be drowning at the shallow end of a municipal swimming pool. In the early years, we would hang big water bags from the olive tree at the end of the terrace and shower underneath them, with views of the sea. We created our own hot water by wrapping these bags in black plastic and putting them out on the roof every morning. By evening we would have hot water. If it was mid August, and the day had been fiercely hot, the water was sometimes even too hot.

Our shower system works well, unless one of your essential joys in life is to submerge in a bath filled with gallons of hot water. For guests like these a good alternative is the sea, just twenty minutes' walk away; or better still, the freshwater creek, where the salt content is low. Now we have a 'proper' shower and sink, but still use the same basic system for hot water, with one or more black bags on the roof immediately above and connected to the shower head with a length of pipe. A proper cold water system ending in a tap at a sink or basin, would require a tank in the roof and a pump to fill it with water from the *sterna*.

After some research I found an Italian-made rotary hand pump which would lift water from twenty feet below and deliver it up a further forty feet, if necessary, to a tank which we had placed in the apex of the olive press roof. The specified rate of flow was ten gallons per minute, so the pumping time required each day would be quite short for our modest requirements. Mark and I mounted the pump on a suitable piece of timber, and from the *sterna*, connected the lower pipe with its filter and non-return valve. Once we had done this we were ready to connect the upper pipe as soon as water started to flow, but despite vigorous pumping not a drop of water emerged. Only one of us was an engineer, so I asked Mark what he had done wrong.

'You're the one who bought the thing, not me,' he said.

We took off the plate; everything seemed fine. We examined the filter, which looked OK to me. Then Mark looked at the non-return valve.

'Did you put this on? It's the wrong way round! No wonder the water couldn't get through.' He started to reverse the valve and I disappeared swiftly to fetch us a drink and avoid further questions of competence.

The pump worked beautifully. We fixed a float in the upper tank and made an indicator for the water level with a stick and a piece of string. We used ordinary garden hosepipe to bring the water down to the sink. When the tank was full, we turned on the tap and after a half a minute of gurgling, rushes of air and silence, there was a sudden gulp, then a whoosh of water shot into the basin. It was a miracle of nineteenth-century plumbing, without the lead pipes. Mark and I had a celebration: no more work for the day.

The hosepipe worked until the winter. We discovered the problem the following summer on our return when we tried to re-start the system. Rats, like crafty computer hackers, had 'entered' our system in about twenty different places, searching for drops of water. In one place the pipe had been completely severed, and every pipe needed replacing. This time we chose a simpler route, so that it could all be more easily dismantled for safe storage in the winter. Overall the manual pump has been a success; but the simplest and quickest way of getting five litres of water from the *sterna* is still just to drop in a bucket and pull it up.

At the beginning of June one year, I arrived at the olive press to find there was no water. The *sterna* was almost empty. Sandra and Daisy were due to join me in ten days, and two weeks later Lucy and Charlie would arrive with Tilly, our first grandchild, aged two. All this would be impossible without water. I flashed a torch into the *sterna* and could see a hole in the side near the bottom. Strong roots from the olive tree behind had broken through the cement. I removed the headstone at the top of the *sterna*, lowered a ladder and climbed down to check other possible points of leakage lightly tapping the surfaces and listening for places where cement had become detached from the stone behind. A good friend, Makis, came to help break open the cracks in order to cut back the roots and then refill with cement. He said he feared they would break through again in a year or two.

I thought hard to find options for water, but finally there was only one practical resolution, which was possible, which might work and which had certainly never been tried before in the three hundred or so years of history at the olive press. I drove into town and bought 800 metres of flexible plastic pipe, in fifty metre lengths, together with sixteen connectors, which would surely have been immediately rejected by any prudent water engineer. The driver of the local water delivery tanker, Spiro, agreed to bring his lorry to the nearest point on the hill above the olive press. Makis returned to help connect the pipes as best we could and then we laid them all the way from the top of the hill down to the olive press and into the *sterna*. Spiro connected the first pipe to his water tank and turned on the tap. The pipe, which had come flat for easy handling, swelled up as the water shot through it down the hillside. I followed it down the hill checking the connectors, which were all holding well except at the point where the pipe turned up the slope from the mule track to the olive press. Here the extra pressure was causing water to burst from a connector into the hillside at violent speed. We managed to fit two extra grips, only to move the pressure point back up the pipe, where a section suddenly blew up to the size of a football. We could do nothing but hope. I imagined thousands of litres of water running to waste down the thirsty hillside. But the pipe held. It was wonderful to hear water gushing into the *sterna*. Half the world, which is short of water, will understand how I felt to see the level gradually rising in the *sterna*; it took an hour to store away, in safety, four thousand precious litres. Makis and I spent the rest of the day disconnecting and rolling up the pipes, to keep in case of future need. I was finished at six o'clock and took a shower; the best I have ever had.

Another useful piece of equipment, which we bought for just twenty-five pounds, is the washing machine – manual, of course. It is a sturdy plastic sphere, about the size of a large beach ball, with a screw top lid like a pressure cooker, a stand and a detachable handle. By rotating the handle steadily to turn the drum you can wash a load of two double sheets in a couple of minutes! My family is amused at my enthusiasm for it. But the best part is choosing where we want to do the washing. Which view would be most pleasing on a particular morning? Would it be shade or sunshine, sea or hillside or both, the mountains or the olive grove, or the garden perhaps?

There are always other earthly matters of concern. The loo arrangements are primitive. Without water, normal sanitation is difficult. There are toilets that recycle water, like those used in aircraft; but they need electricity and disposal arrangements. Deep pits can be used but not here, not unless you dynamite great holes in the rock. The best option for now are chemical camping loos, which use minimal water, but require periodic burials on the hillside. Needless to say this job is generally delegated to me. Later, we'll have to build a sceptic tank and lay proper drain-pipes.

You won't be surprised to hear that there was no refuse collection here, so we recycled as much as possible and divided other rubbish into three categories. Anything burnable goes up in smoke from the fireplace. Discarded vegetable material and anything else which rots was put in a small bright metal dustbin, for dehydration and composting, safe from the attention of rats but popular with wasps. Metal and glass were then the only materials remaining, for disposal at the rubbish tip near the village. This involved a difficult drive along a narrow one-way track that led round the edge of a steep hill, to a point where a wider area has been carved out to form part of the dump. Most of the rubbish is shot over the precipice along the outer edge. On one visit, I found the whole area covered with rubbish, leaving no space for turning the camping van and forcing a risky reverse journey for more than a mile, back to the road.

The problem of rats is one which, like most people, I prefer not to discuss. For two years I got away with calling them squirrels – after all they did like climbing through trees. No other wild creature of that size is clever enough to live a free independent life in such close proximity to mankind; in London, it's said that you are never more than eight feet away from one. When the squirrel argument became no longer plausible, I called them country rats, like Ratty in The Wind in the Willows – not quite squirrels, but surely nothing to worry about. But if you think of them slinking up from city sewers, flicking the rubbery flesh of their long hairless tails and feeling their way past you at night with furtive noses and whiskers, you reach desperately for poison, guns, traps, cats, dogs. The Venetians faced the same problem, five hundred years ago, when a plague of rats afflicted the Ionian islands. They came up with a good solution. They imported large numbers of cats from Syria into the islands and passed two new laws. One, under pain of death, no one may harm these cats. Two, under pain of death, no one may feed these cats. The rat population declined very rapidly in response to this early example of biological control.

At the olive press we have no cats or dogs or guns. We protect pipes, bags and equipment as much as possible, but rats will get through almost anything if they really try. And other than stoic acceptance, poison is the only remedy. Most rat poisons now act, in part, like super effective sleeping pills and allegedly cause no pain. The only problem occurs if you find an apparently dead rat, lying on the ground; you pick it up for burial and find that the poison hasn't yet completed its task. The rat fights like a tiger to stay awake and to stay alive. It has happened twice now and it's unpleasant and hard to kill them. Then you bury the body and call out to the others, 'Don't die on the terrace or in other obvious places.'

*

A friend of ours from London, James, happened to be sailing out to the islands to coincide with our first summer at Margarita's olive press. We took the opportunity to ask him to bring out a couple of items which we naively considered to be a priority for our first summer: a wheelbarrow and a chemical toilet. It soon became apparent however, that the wheelbarrow was useless over the steep rocky surfaces of the hillside and the porta potti was attacked by rats, who discovered fresh water in the upper compartment and bit through the plastic to reach it. The following year James, our very dashing deliveryman, brought out a gas fridge for us and a small fibreglass boat. I had last used it on the river Mole in Surrey, where I had rented an isolated fifteenth-century cottage for almost twenty years from a generous landlord for one pound a week. James kindly put the fridge in his rubber boat, tied our fibreglass dinghy behind and set off from Kefallonia, at high speed no doubt, in the direction of the Zakynthos coast and our local taverna. More than halfway across, he looked back and saw the rope trailing in the water, like a slipped tether, my boat nowhere to be seen. He turned back, he said, but could find nothing. Despite its beauties the river Mole could readily be exchanged for the Ionian sea, and Kefallonia is certainly preferable to Gatwick but I like to think that my boat still sails free on the Ionian sea, like a rider-less horse making its escape. More likely, local fishermen had captured the boat and were now working it harder than ever before.

The story of the fridge was more prosaic. It didn't work. James and I had carried it, step by step, up the hillside and finally located it beside a gas cylinder that we had brought up in an equally painful process. After further effort and patience the pilot light ignited and heat emerged from the little chimney. Nothing else happened. Beer and wine were not cooled. Ice for cool drinks or whisky refused to form. The fridge was designed to run on electricity or gas, so the problem might only have been with the gas. So sometime later Thomas and I carried it, at sunrise, for twenty minutes up the mule track to the house at the top, which has electricity. Three days later there was still no discernable change in temperature, so we brought it back to the olive press. Somebody said it could certainly be sorted out in town, so on another early morning we took it down the hill and drove into town to find a friend of Lambis' who was an expert on fridges. He worked for a couple of hours and declared it kaput, because the refrigerant was exhausted.

We left it on a dump and resolved to try again the following year.

I tend to rise early and get the day's domestic activities done before the rest of the family are up. These morning jobs usually end with the house electrics. Our prime source of electric light is a lantern with a fluorescent tube and a battery charged by a solar generator about the size of a briefcase. This folds open like a book and is placed on the roof, until the sun drops behind the mountains in the late afternoon. The most important advantage of the solar panel is its silence; even a 'quiet' diesel electric generator would thump out its message over the whole hillside whenever it was on. Through a transformer the solar generator charges all our batteries, for everything from our reading lights to Daisy's walkman. We have a couple of other lights and a fluorescent torch with their own solar charging panels. These are used for background lighting or emergencies but the light they give is harsh and blue. Our system is small and flexible and well suited to our present migratory habits. Later, when we plan to spend longer periods here, decisions will be needed about whether to invest in a larger solar electric system or explore the possibilities of bringing down an electric cable from our neighbours at the top. Then we could have switches and pay electricity bills like everybody else.

9

Fish Taverna
Fishing, cooking and pouring the wine

I have good memories of staying a week at Nionio's fish taverna in the early days when no part of the olive press was habitable. The small fishing community there had remained untouched, more or less, for centuries living on as the world around it changed.

A dusty road leads down to the little peninsular, where half a dozen houses surround the taverna. A fishing boat, the Saint Barbara, is moored beside the smooth slabs of rock in front, where the nets are stretched out to dry. In the boat, a white canopy gives shade to the pale blue wheelhouse and the deck. The wooden hull has been carefully painted in white and is lapped by the friendly movements of the sea. Close to the shore, the *micro nisi* floats like an upturned saucer, motionless on the dark blue sea. Shrubs, evergreen and ochre, sprouting oregano and dried grasses break up the rocky surface. Wild black rabbits inhabit this inhospitable little island, with no predators apart from Nionio, who owns the island, making occasional hunting expeditions when demanded by the taverna menu. At other times and with binoculars, the rabbits can be seen hopping about quietly between the rocks, even from as far away as our olive press.

It was already late for a lunchtime meal when I arrived to stay; Nionio was about to settle down for the afternoon siesta, which he takes on a long wooden bench in the main part of the restaurant. He would have been out in the early hours of the morning to catch the fish needed in the taverna for lunch and other meals until midday tomorrow. Nionio has a lovely family name, Pyromalis, but most people called him by his nickname Kokkinos, meaning red. When he was younger his hair had been red; now it is white and crinkly. Once his eyes would have been the colour of the Ionian, I think, now they are pale blue, sun bleached by years of working on the glaring water. I asked him once whether his nickname had political connotations, prompting him to throw up his hands in mock horror, 'We never have politics here.'

When Nionio sleeps, Diamanto shuffles around like an ageing mother superior, weary and a little down at heel. She is unsmiling most of the time, but you should catch her when she does smile, a little hesitant and shy, with a sudden spark of light in her sleepy brown eyes. Would I like whitebait, a *choriatiki* (country salad), chips and white wine *apo vareli* (from the cask)? Would I like the fish to be cooked on the charcoal grill? I have had lobster, crab, squid and octopus, mullet, mackerel, cuttlefish; the list is seemingly inexhaustible. A favourite dish of Diamanto is fried aubergine, sliced very thinly and crisp on the edges.

'*Melitzanes tiganites*,' she told me, 'depend on preparation, but are quite simple.'

She became more friendly and less shy as we talked. 'The aubergines are sliced very thinly, salted and left for at least an hour; then I wash them thoroughly and drain. Cooking is easy; just dip them in flour and fry in olive oil. Before serving, drain them and add a little more salt. Sometimes I make a tomato sauce and add garlic and oregano. The only other secret is to use our own olive oil.' We bring back bottles of the island's olive oil every year to see us through the winter months in London.

That first evening and for the rest of the week, I was the only visitor staying at the taverna, and at meal-times I sat at Nionio's and Diamanto's table with one of their daughters, who would soon be leaving the family household to be married. Every evening we had fish soup, partly saved from monotony by the inclusion of different fish. We would also watch a Greek TV soap series on an ancient black and white television, which, like the fish soup, changed little from one episode to the next.

People go to bed late and rise early here. I was awoken before five each day, by the declining phut-phut of a moped outside my room, doubtless bringing a crew member for the fishing boat. Noisy banging would break away remaining bits of barnacle and rubbish still carried in the nets. One man had a well-developed sense of humour and his laughter alone could have kept the world awake. Eventually the diesel motor would thud into action, the odd shout, then off to work, and to the open sea.

Nionio goes out in his boat less frequently now, leaving most of the fishing to his son Spiro and giving himself more time for running the taverna. Now that the road, which I call *dromo pyromali*, is surfaced all the way from the village, business is more active during the tourist months. From time to time a few visitors arrive, having been misled by a road sign higher up the hill, implying that the famous blue caves are best visited from here, actually three times as far by boat as from the main starting point further up the coast. No language, other than Greek, is spoken at the taverna and misunderstandings are rife. My own contribution as an interpreter usually helps to intensify the confusion and the fun.

Certainly I was made very welcome. My bedroom was a separate building attached to the taverna, like a small chapel, with a huge iron bedstead in place of an altar. The taverna itself is a wide interior space supported by exposed concrete pillars. The sea wraps around you on two sides, exposed by enormous plate glass windows. Below the window is a narrow terrace, shaded by a trailing vine, with a 10-metre fall of rock descending to the sea below. For years local authorities disputed whether laws were infringed when the front of the taverna was built so close to the sea, but no such concerns affect passers-by, who wonder at the panorama and dine on the freshest fish in Europe. How many restaurants still have their own fishing boat or can choose when they want their fish to be landed?

From the cool of the taverna you see the land reach gently down to the coast and sweep around a large craggy bay. Northwards, beyond rocky headlands, another small island is visible with a ruined monastery close to the water. According to local history, this is still owned by the Vatican, having been forgotten in the treaties that marked the end of the Venetian Empire. It provides a fine sheltered haven, in bad weather, for boats anchored in the harbour. The last great headland to the north marks the beginning of the *galatsies spilies*, the blue caves, where white limestone rock has been eroded into archways and caves by a brilliant turquoise sea. The unique clarity of the seas around the island is perfected here. Beyond the headland, the high mountains of Kefallonia are prominent in clear weather, or become disembodied peaks, separated from their earthbound foothills by thick white puffs of cloud.

These are the fixed unchanging realities of the panorama through the windows of the fish taverna. But changing light from sunrise to evening imposes its own reality, and the sea, which alone joins the separate parts, is itself the most changeable part of all. The view impresses me every time, particularly after another year away, when so many things have changed elsewhere and nothing has changed here.

Local people come down at lunch-time. Before the surfacing of the road, the taverna was frequented only by an occasional tractor driver, people on mopeds and others driving precarious three-wheeled agricultural vans, which are always painted green and struggle not to topple on the hairpin bends. One Sunday we came down from the olive press for a late lunch to find that tables had been put together along the whole length of the restaurant and everyone was singing in a rhythmic, almost choral unison. I asked Nionio if they were singing folk songs or love songs.

'They are singing patriotic songs from the island,' he replied.

The room was filled with a rhythm and a surge, as from the sea. Older people, teenagers and children all sang together. Amid this outburst of patriotism, I remembered Margarita with a smile. *Xeni sto fourno* – foreigners into the oven!

Once the new road had made the taverna more accessible, a feast was arranged for local politicians from this and neighbouring islands. Behind the main table, a large number of local people were crammed into extra tables, with more standing. After the lengthy and enjoyable meal had come to an end, the politicians stood up to leave, and were descended upon, within seconds and from every direction. Requests, petitions, roads, boundaries, electricity supplies, mooring rights, access, entitlements to subsidies, tax problems; a cornucopia of hopeful appeals. The hunting season had commenced, following an expensive meal for which the hunted were now paying dearly.

*

Nionio has been interested and amused by the different 'workers' and relatives who have joined me over the years to help at the olive press. Thomas was the first and has remained his favourite; most years, he asks for news of him. It impresses me, especially as an aspiring linguist, that they had no common language and yet had managed to communicate so well. On one occasion I told Nionio that my Greek teacher in London, who is a charming and lively Athenian woman called Hero, wanted to come out and help me with rebuilding one of the roofs. Nionio reflected a moment and said,

'I don't think the roof would make much progress, but you would certainly enjoy improving your Greek.'

The roof is now restored; my Greek slowly gets better, though imperceptibly. Years later, Nionio remembered our exchange about the roof; ancient blue eyes flickered for a moment, 'I love women,' he said, 'I don't remember why.'

Our friend, James, was a marine biologist and a regular visitor to the *psari* taverna, usually arriving, with much noise and flair, in his high-powered rubber boat from Kefallonia. And the summer that my friend Brian stayed at the taverna was the year that James brought the mermaids. They arrived at dusk in a double-masted schooner. From the windows of the taverna he could be seen far out at sea, approaching with a full set of sails, heading towards the *micro nisi*. The sails came down as he rounded the point of the island, entered the bay and anchored midway between the island and the shore. A ramp was lowered at the stern and we saw James powering towards the rocks below the taverna in a speedboat. He had brought with him twenty American girls who were studying marine biology. They were to spend a couple of days anchored here before sailing south down the eastern coast of the island. Later they came ashore for an evening meal. The taverna had never seen anything like it.

Nionio discovered some common language and engaged in deep discussions at preferred tables. Diamanto came to life for a few hours as an active mother superior exercising traditional custody over her community. James sat at the head of the longest table, heroically claiming attention. He talked about the turtles around the island and the marine world that he had known for almost ten years. 'At this end of the island,' he was saying, 'you can still occasionally come across seals. The fishermen hate them, for eating the fish. In Greek they are called *fokya.*'

There was a pause and from over the table, in a slow southern American accent came, 'That's what I've been looking for since I got here.'

Laughter sparkled like a shoal of flying fish over the table. James seemed to reach for the oxygen cylinder and carried on.

'They're called Monk seals.'

'Now you tell me,' sighed the same girl with a look that guaranteed her clandestine entry, any night, to a monastery of her choice.

James ignored her with growing interest and continued, 'Not only do they eat the fish, they also break into the fishermen's nets where they can be certain of finding plenty of fish. Monk seals are very rare; it's thought that only about a thousand still exist in the Mediterranean and off the Atlantic coast of Morocco. They are greyish brown in colour, sometimes white, and larger than ordinary grey seals.'

'Larger?' she said. 'That's good.' Nothing is safe from innuendo, once the idea takes hold. Everybody laughed.

'I prefer mermaids to Monk seals,' said James.

'Take me,' she paused, 'for a swim.'

But James had already started on his next subject.

'Marine turtles are found among all the Ionian Islands, but particularly Kefallonia and Zakynthos; they're called Loggerhead turtles. They live like amphibious tortoises and breathe air like mammals. Very seldom do they come ashore, but when you see one, at night, shuffling very slowly up a beach to lay her eggs, or when you find one swimming near the surface of the sea, 140kg in weight and up to a metre long, apparently defenceless, it's hard to believe that you are watching one of the most successful species ever to have evolved in the history of the world. They were around at the time of the dinosaurs. Their species has lived on earth for a hundred million years. Now they are under threat, by man of course, in the sea and on the beaches where they breed; man is surely the only predator capable of destroying, in a generation, a hundred million years of evolution.'

The girl said nothing; perhaps she was getting a different perspective. The rest of the taverna was quiet; everybody listened.

Then she asked, 'How did they survive so long?'

'That's even more surprising. Their life cycle and reproduction arrangements are extremely hazardous. They live for sixty or seventy years but take between twenty and forty years to reach maturity. It is believed that a female turtle returns to lay her eggs on the same beach where she herself was hatched out, perhaps forty years before. But it has not been proved. She digs a nest in the sand about half way up the beach, lays approximately a hundred eggs, and completes the operation up to four times in a season. From the possible four hundred eggs, only one or two will survive to breed again at least twenty years later. With those systems and equipment, how could the species have survived for a hundred million years? You don't need a statistician to confirm that luck is not a factor over such a period! And what scientist would describe it simply as a will to live?'

'I have that,' she said.

'You'll need more than that.'

'Is there more?' she asked.

Margarita's Olive Press

James said he would fetch the boat to return everybody to the schooner. The girl left with him. Later, lights could be seen on board the schooner; then they vanished.

'Does that mean we get the boat later or sooner?' somebody asked.

Nionio muttered an opinion in Greek that nobody understood until they saw Diamanto smiling away the forty years of hard labour that crossed and creased her face. The party continued into the early morning.

*

My friend Brian, in London, told me that the 'real' Greece doesn't exist any more.

'There's still Greek culture of course, but the rest is just tourism and business.' I persuaded him to spend ten days at the *psari* taverna. He hoped it might be a good place to write poetry. He was given the same room where I had stayed and every morning at five am experienced the same dawn chorus. During the day he would write in the shade of the vine on the terrace, until he noticed three empty shower cubicles by the beach. These are set into rocks at the back of the shore, with open fronts facing the sea. Each has a shower head and Nionio turns on the main tap, in the summer, if there is water to spare. Brian moved a chair and small table to the middle cubicle and wrote, surrounded by concrete on five sides and by the *micro nisi*, the sea and the mountains on the other. A couple of years later a book of his poems was published and he very kindly gave me a copy but never said if any had come from the

120

bunker, opposite the *micro nisi*. Brian never came back, perhaps due to a wrecked knee from a near fatal odyssey at midday, on the mountain, searching for Margarita's olive press. No doubt about that Greek reality then.

I love the *psari* taverna for remaining unchanged over the years. Some new building work has taken place; the generator and freezer were probably installed ten or fifteen years ago, but essentially all is the same as it always was. The relaxed and sometimes absent service is probably the same now as when Diamanto and Nionio were young. Certainly I am glad not to be professionally engaged as their management consultant. The place could be made more efficient and profitable in a month, transforming the atmosphere from tranquillity to bustle. First, Diamanto would have to go and be replaced by a high-powered multilingual chef who can produce authentic Greek menus in four languages. Nionio would have a public relations role, taking children out in his boat round the *micro nisi*, chatting up customers, telling of his life as a fisherman. The interior would be given a face-lift, by replacing the faded Charlie's Angels posters, bare concrete floors and redundant fishing tackle with hand-woven rugs and fisherman's lamps. Prices could double, at least in the tourist season, profits would more than quadruple and another charming spot of 'the old Greece' would be gone forever. Perhaps all would change except the sea.

10

Swimming
Discover a perfect beach and keep it secret…

At the tiny cove nearest to the olive press, high cliffs plunge down into a green transparent sea. We call it the Butterfly Beach, or sometimes – the Margarita Beach. Over the years we have delighted in exploring the pebbled coves at the north of island, joyfully discovering the best spots for picnicking, or swimming. We like to take our time, for the tranquillity and beauty of a good beach is usually incompatible with tourists and other intruders.

We first visited the beach by boat. In those early days we had a system whereby, at the end of every holiday, each of us would choose one dream day for a favourite activity or pass-time. The only rule was that the others had to participate. Daisy would generally choose imaginative options, like making us all swim out to a raft for breakfast, or spending all day on a pedalo boat eating nothing but ice creams, so we learnt to let her have her day when we were both feeling energetic. My choice had been to hire a boat and come with a picnic to the Margarita beach.

That day there was no breeze and no ripples on the surface of the water. We could see through to the rocks and plants on the sea-bed, as if the water hardly existed. In such transparency our little boat felt suspended, floating as in mid air. Gradually we neared the tiny crescent of the Butterfly Beach and crunched up onto smooth white shingle. Ahead a narrow valley climbs its way up through the hillside, providing a channel for winter rain down to the sea. Higher up we could see a cluster of cypress trees, which we knew later as the 'garden of cypresses'. One side of the Butterfly beach offers morning shade, until the sun moves round, and leaves the other side in shade. That first afternoon we spent hours swimming, reading, enjoying a picnic and a siesta afterwards, sunbathing, exploring. This is the general pattern of life at the Butterfly Beach. And nobody else in the world is here.

We seldom find anybody in this beautiful cove, but try not to develop a sense of ownership. Our growing conviction that nobody else ever came here was upset one year when a party of Greeks arrived in a rubber boat and camped on the beach for a couple of nights. When this happened we found ourselves in the extraordinary position of resenting the presence of Greeks on one of their own islands! They too seemed a little resentful of foreigners, perhaps with more reason. I said we lived here, just up the hill. The more we talked the more our mutual resentments evaporated. It is best, perhaps, to think of everything as leasehold, nothing freehold.

From the Butterfly Beach you can swim round to a larger cove, another of the pebbled inlets that stretch along this part of the island's coast. Here fishermen once pulled their boats up the shore, using the winch that now stands rusting at the back of the beach. Local people, coming to collect fish, would have ridden their donkeys down a track that is now badly overgrown, to see what was on offer. Fishermen setting out on long trips would have been able to fill their bottles from the nearby well, which provides fresh water throughout the year. Fish can now be bought only at the taverna or at the next village. But the Winch Beach remains a good place for a swim.

*

At the taverna there are two good places for swimming, one on either side of the narrow peninsula. Mark usually launches his surfboard from the rocks in front of the taverna, stepping straight onto it regardless, it seems, of prevailing winds, gales or sea conditions that sometimes threaten to wreck the stout board, let alone the more vulnerable body. There are plenty of places for diving and one spot where flat sloping rocks allow a more gentle pedestrian entry to the sea. The *micro nisi* can be reached with a brisk swim, but its rocks are very sharp, protecting the rabbit paradise from unwelcome visitors. The showers at the back of the beach and the luxuries of fresh food and cold beer in the taverna make this site an easy swimming option for building workers from the hillside.

Being holiday folk just looking to relax for the day, we head to the freshwater inlet on the other side of the peninsula, where there is a small jetty for fishing boats, and a sheltered harbour. Here we are close enough to the taverna for refreshments; there is occasional boating activity to watch and a few children swim at the miniature beach at the head of the inlet; opposite and behind are the mountains. On a hot day, this is perfect swimming; fresh water springs or underground streams cool and dilute the salt content of the sea, so the water is usually calm and fresh.

Wide smooth slabs of rock cater ideally for the most important part of life on the beach – the lazy part. The rocks we swim from lean back against the sheer drop of a hillside, which has eroded away at sea level to expose great expanses of rose coloured crystal. When Daisy was little she would pretend she was mining diamonds, and gather up carefully chosen collections of the best stones on a beach mat, to shine in the sun. You can dive in from the little jetty and swim around the fishing boats or over to the rocks opposite, or, carefully avoiding the black sea-urchins that threaten bare feet, you can take the rocky route in from the shore. This is a place that sees the recent past surrender to the present, forcing you to shake off more of life's other concerns with every hour that potters by.

*

The fifth place to swim is just as beautiful but busier. Locals call it *Makriyalou*, the Far Beach. Once reached by a narrow coastal track beyond the *psari* taverna, it stretches out for about a quarter of a mile, surrounded by high cliffs on all sides. This was the first beach at our end of the island where we were able to buy ice cream. Panaiotis and his brother, the entrepreneurial nephews of my old friend Dionysius, set up the first beach bar there and we would sometimes take the boat round to buy ice creams or drinks. Now on the high cliffs behind, there's another taverna which was originally and suitably named 'the Paradise Bar'.

Tourist boats sometimes arrive from the town and local visitors arrive by car from the northern end of the island where there is no other comparable beach. The atmosphere is quite different from the other bays, where we generally swim alone. This is a Greek beach in a beautiful setting, not usually overcrowded, but busy enough – typical, in the summer season, of many such special places throughout Greece. Panaiotis and his brother had a difficult task running their bar. Everything had to be carried here over a long dusty journey; their generator had to be kept going at all costs, or full loads of ice cream would perish and food stocks for snacks would have to be jettisoned. But still they found time and energy for gardening and planted oleanders and mini cypress trees in olive oil tins filled with earth and placed along the front of the bar; a bougainvillea was started on the side of their little hut. They opened all summer, at all hours, and one of them usually slept there. The season of comfort, for them, was the winter, which after a long summer they gladly anticipated and certainly deserved.

From *Makriyalou* you could see a dust track winding up above the beach and higher around the cliffs behind, heading along the coast to the south. At that time all the maps showed a road along the coast, but anyone who ever tried it sooner or later came to a halt in the middle of nowhere. Now a new road has been completed, and our end of the island has gradually become more readily accessible to tourist invasions in the holidays and to local people at normal times.

After three years' trading, Panaiotis and his brother were told that their bar was on someone else's land. It was quickly pulled down and a more commercial enterprise set up further from the beach.

*

One year Lambis and I took a dawn tour of the beaches in the North.

'It's time I made a visit of inspection at the colony,' he said one day. The 'colony' was how he described the olive press and its surrounding buildings. The last time Lambis had visited was years before, when he had brought Spiro to advise on the new roof structure after the snowstorm. I offered to collect him from his house behind the fig tree beach, but he disliked driving his car on the corniche road with its hairpin bends and precipitous edges and preferred the slower lumbering safety and high visibility of the buses. He arrived up at the village, at six in the morning, but was sprightly even at that hour, saying, 'We must treat this as a proper military operation. The entire area from here to the sea must be captured and commanded.' It was the kind of game we both enjoyed, and for which we were far too old.

'Our resources are small, but with determination…'

We were passing through the first small hamlet of scattered houses, down the hill from the village. All doors and shutters were closed. We saw nobody.

'Report back, Rodney, captured with no resistance.' I made the required radio report, and we drove on.

'We shall have to go down to the beaches. There are at least three possible landing areas where we might meet stiff resistance.' More to the point, it would delay our arrival at the colony.

'It could be tougher there.'

Finally we drove past the *psari* taverna and the *micro nisi* and along to *Makriyalou*, where the little bar was shut and nobody could be seen in any direction.

'Another easy victory,' said Lambis.

We walked down to the sea and skimmed smooth flat stones over the calm almost motionless water. I managed four jumps; Lambis did six. It was certainly his day

.

We drove back to the *psari* taverna. Nionio was out on his fishing boat and everyone else had gone back to sleep. No hostile landings could be detected.

'Let's go and look at the Margarita beach,' I said. We parked in our usual spot, where the footpath to the olive press reached the track, and walked down to the cove.

'During the war,' said Lambis, 'there were stories that British submarines picked up or landed people in isolated creeks, like this, at the northern end of the island. Maybe here!'

Lambis started to pick up stones from the beach – for more skimming over the water, I thought but he put them in a plastic bag and said, 'No other beach on the island has so many perfectly smooth round stones.'

'Do you collect them, General ?' I asked, in line with the morning's fantasy. Perhaps he had a special catapult.

'It's the best way of killing snakes,' he replied. So he did have a catapult. 'If they are really smooth and round, and the right size, snakes think they are eggs and swallow them. These stones are ideal.' He then started to cluck like a chicken; it was most infectious and I joined him a few moments later. Humour and madness are sometimes difficult to separate. No doubt about our action – a certain madness. We collected a full bag of stones and agreed it was the most useful military achievement of the morning so far.

By then it was half past eight and a good time to start walking up the hill to the olive press. Sandra and Daisy had been up for half an hour; the breakfast table was laid and coffee was on its way. Lambis reported to Sandra, 'The whole area surrendered without resistance.'

'Even on the beaches,' I added.

She was right to think that strong coffee and something to eat would swiftly restore us to the real world.

11

Daily Life
Slow down, do tomorrow, be today

Life on the island finds its own pace. We fill our days with simple things, swimming, walks along the coast, a boat trip to find melons or feta pies, searching the hillside for new wild flowers to catalogue. Every day brings something different and, most of all, the slowing down to enjoy the natural rhythm of life.

The day opens with breakfast. We gather on the terrace, helping ourselves to Greek yoghurt with peaches or grapes, fresh orange juice, black coffee and bread with scented local honey or even home made damson jam from Suffolk. Those who arrive late sit facing the olive press building, but first comers, on the other side of the table, can look down the hill and see through the olive trees, to the sea, shining in the morning sun. On the right a great carob tree, loaded with little black bananas, offers more sweetness in this gentle land. We have spent many happy hours at the long wooden table on the terrace, which now looks very much at home. I built it in England from two pine planks taken from work surfaces in the dairy of a 16th-century farmhouse where we live in Suffolk. The table is therefore a gift to an ancient Greek olive press from an old English farmhouse, none the less sincere for the imperfect quality of the carpentry.

Breakfast is such a pleasant daily happening that it risks endless extension from the early morning onwards towards lunchtime. As the sun climbs, the shade stays with us on the terrace and the breeze rising from the coast remains cool. The passing minutes are measured by what you should be doing instead and enjoyed still more. Jobs done early in the morning are forgotten.

Between two olive trees on the lower terrace is the Mexican hammock, which is woven in cotton and coloured in three shades of blue, straight from the sea. Sometimes a book is taken from the breakfast table and the reader becomes freely submerged for hours in the gentle ocean swell of Mexican indolence. The temptation can be avoided only by letting someone else climb in first. For the more active, there is the swing that hangs from an olive branch at the front edge of the lower terrace. The wooden seat was originally used by a fisherman for winding his line through the deep 'V' shaped cuts at each end. These cuts serve equally well for holding the rope from the bough above. When the greenhouse effect has done its worst and the seas rise, I imagine the wooden seat floating away, probably to be found once more by a fisherman and set back to work, just like my little boat which floated free from James somewhere between here and Kefallonia.

Sit and hold the ropes; kick off from the stone wall below and the ground immediately drops to the terrace of the next pathway below; as rhythm and speed increase the ground falls again beyond the further edge of the path and lies more than ten metres below. The *micro nisi* and the rest of the world are below. Ahead the sea and sky meet at the horizon. No other people or houses can be seen, just occasionally a boat. But as you begin to think this is your domain, the spell is broken. At best, you are the part and it the whole. The swing is long and high. Try to reach up to olive branches with your feet. At night, you touch the stars.

When breakfast is considered well and truly over and washing up completed with a cupful of water, the day's vacation can begin. Even building work is deferred, endless swimming things are gathered up and we potter off down the hill, lapsing meanwhile into a discussion of where we would like to go.

*

The local shop is the main meeting point in the village, where people come to drink coffee, play cards and chat about the happenings of the day. On a good day Iannis would have exactly what you are looking for; on a bad day and late in the afternoon, food supplies run low and the best has already gone. But by the following morning when local supplies came in, a feast of fresh fruit and vegetables are piled high again in wooden and plastic boxes, on the floor, beside his counter and all around the room. Flaky pale brown onions, large red misshapen Mediterranean tomatoes, long flat tender green beans, chubby courgettes, many with their pale yellow flowers still attached, aubergines like fat shiny cardinals splendidly purple. Everything has a price, which is sometimes marked but usually not. Iannis knows them all.

On some days there are trays of peaches, which often need to ripen a day or two more before you can bite into them and feel them melt away into streams of juice. A small cool counter carries local cheese, feta and yoghurts. Often there are packets of bacon, unmistakably labelled in English 'Piggy Bacon,' and melons and grapes, later in the summer. Sometimes as we were leaving, Iannis give us a bottle of his own dry white wine.

In the past, it was Iannis' father who looked after the shop. He would chat to the customers about everyday things with a light-hearted humour that made him many friends in the village. In London, one autumn, I heard from Lambis that he had died suddenly. In my mind, he was associated for so long with one particular location that I feared returning to the empty shop the following year. I immediately wrote to Iannis, though my Greek, I think, failed the test. The 'I will miss him' that I intended, became, 'He will miss me.' An odd thing to say in a letter of condolence, though his father, who always had a robust sense of humour, might have smiled posthumously.

In the lower village, you can buy bread and sweet cakes with syrup and nuts from the bakery, and as you leave the road is lined with colourful rugs and lacework, hanging from stalls to tempt passers by. Great expanses of cream and white lace remind tourists of their duty to return with souvenirs, intricately patterned bedspreads are strung up to catch the eye of newly-weds or lovers. The workmanship, if the word can be used to cover the exclusive work of women, is careful and endlessly repetitive. Panel after panel emerges, day after day, night after night, unerringly put together to create an heirloom for richer people to buy and, surely, treasure.

One afternoon I headed to the carpenter's workshop in the village with a handsaw that needed sharpening. While there, I discovered that the carpenter's wife spent her days weaving. I was invited to see the room where she worked the loom, shining and polished smooth by generations of labour. He agreed that I could return with Sandra to see the loom in operation. It clacked and thumped; a hypnotic blend of noise and motion mesmerised the eyes and ears. Strands of wool were seemingly thrown in every direction; the smell of wool and sheep was potent and all around. Among the rugs that she had made was a long runner with horizontal strands of blues and white, blurred, like the meeting of sea with foam. It was too long for where we wanted to use it. Would it be spoilt if divided into two smaller rugs?

'No, of course not,' she smiled, 'it might even be better. Just give me time to finish the edges properly.'

We returned the following day and bought the pair of beautiful rugs. They differ from each other like moments on the sea.

*

Only occasionally is the serenity interrupted, usually by fate or chance. Early in our visits to the island, I unwittingly gave Sandra a terrible shock as she was enjoying beach life with Daisy. They were having their last swim of the afternoon when I arrived on my moped, back from negotiations in Zakynthos town, covered in blood. I had met a car cutting across one of the hairpins at high speed and been forced into a simple choice. Car or rocks. Fortunately the precipice was on the other side. I chose the rocks and parted from the bike, which crashed to the ground, leaving the rear wheel spinning furiously. These roads are generally deserted and I was fortunate that another driver came to my rescue with a first aid kit. Meanwhile the racing driver had stopped to see the damage. I thought hard for the words.

'Don't kill all the foreign tourists like this,' I managed to say, 'you badly need their dollars.'

He was astonished and evidently believed I had suffered a nasty knock to the head. I made my way back to meet Sandra and Daisy, decidedly more shaken than I had been when I left in the morning. Sandra cried out in alarm when she saw me. But the injuries were only superficial. They had been treated with red iodine.

*

On the whole life is dictated by the weather, so our days are fairly constant due to unfailing sunshine in the summer months. But if the wind is up, we may decide to take a drive, round to the mountainous cliffs of the west, or the soft sheltered valleys down in the south. Our favourite route leads from our nearest village down through the trees and scrubland in the middle of the island, rejoining the road along the East coast, for an hour of the most spectacular views. We leave the village at the crossroads and drive down the steep mountain ridge to the plateau, passing the craft shops of lace bedspreads and vivid multi-coloured pottery. In July the plateau is a sandy brown colour, having delivered its harvest of grain many weeks before. Beside the road stands an ancient wooden-framed threshing machine, once decorated with bright red paint, now faded and peeling in the heat of summer sunlight. The name 'TITAN' can still be seen on the side, painted in black capital letters, which are the same in Greek as in English. This ageing Titan would have arrived on the mountain roads decades ago, brought in to replace old threshing methods, which had been in use for a thousand years or more. In those days corn sheaves were scattered evenly over circular threshing fields, where mules or horses were tethered to a central pole and galloped round, dragging flails behind them, to take the husks from the grain. These beautiful flat circles are called *aloni*, but like the one we have at the olive press, are now deserted and unused. They can still be seen around the villages to the East and among the fields and hillsides, which stretch down towards the coast.

After about four miles, the plateau comes to an end, where the road turns down through a narrow valley, running between the evergreen mountainsides that are home to herds of black goats. Soon the sea can be glimpsed again, way ahead; the road descends more sharply into long hairpin bends and reveals suddenly, the brilliant 'mid sea blue and shore sea green' of the Ionian. Here the sun is occasionally reflected up from the sea, temporarily blinding the windows of the car with fierce white light. Far below, flat lands surround the seaside village of Alikes, and a strip of golden sand curves around the bay, stretching as far as you can see. Salt has been extracted from these flats continuously for almost five hundred years, since the Venetians set up production in the early fifteen hundreds. Now, because of losses in recent years, the operation is intermittent and alternative tourist projects are under consideration. We wondered if the next project would survive five hundred years.

Eventually the hairpin bends give way, as the road reaches a village and now meanders more calmly past small stone cottages covered with red, white and rare pink bougainvilleas. Here, where water is in plentiful supply, front gardens are lush with oleanders, orange trumpeting campsis, scarlet hibiscus and glorious pale blue plumbago. Once we reach the charming tourist village, further south, we swim and order lunch from one of the many seaside restaurants along the beach, ordering moussaka and Greek salads, hungry after the journey. Before leaving, we stock up on groceries, at what is effectively our nearest supermarket.

If we travel by boat, this journey only takes half an hour in the morning when the sea is usually calm, but longer in the afternoon when the wind gets up and the sea grows rough. In theory a quick shopping trip is possible, were it not for the usual distractions of water-sports and beach-beds. The inevitable late departure makes the ride rough and sometimes alarming; we have even seen the odd pot of yoghurt leap into the sea long before we reach the safety of harbour.

*

In the evenings we return to the olive press, to shower and potter and listen to the radio, or bouzouki music if we are in the mood to dance. Bedtime might be sundown or much later; this is a place that tempts you to live at your own pace. On early nights we prepare our home comforts, reading lights, books and drinks, happy to do without bedroom slippers and fitted carpets. At other times we sip ouzo on the terrace with friends, by the light of gas lamps and candles.

12

Friends and visitors
Philoxenia

We are at home on this lovely hillside, but we are also visitors. So few other visitors reach this remote spot, that those who finally arrive at our house have either been invited with detailed maps and instructions or are just as welcome as rare passers-by who have lost their way. There might have been a notice hung at the top and bottom of the hill, 'Visitors by invitation only,' in Greek and English.

Hospitality, in Greece, is *philoxenia*, keeping the doors of your house open to visitors, and generosity of spirit. During my search I often encountered the kindness of strangers and we would pass this on, now that we had our own home on the island. Our only neighbour, another Dionysius, was our first visitor. To reach us he has to walk all the way from his farmhouse on the northern ridge of the neighbouring valley. He arrived late one afternoon when I was in the hammock, Daisy was on the swing, and Sandra was sitting on the steps preparing some vegetables. He brought with him a large bag of pears freshly picked from a nearby orchard.

Each visitor brings something, fruit or cheese or good conversation, and we in return provide coffee and a warm welcome. In those early years, language was a problem when Dionysius came to visit. I suppose it still is. At one point, he asked whether we had seen rats. I didn't recognise the word. He asked for a piece of paper and a pencil and drew a sketch. The beast looked like a miniature Pterodactyl. We thought it was some kind of bird, an eagle perhaps, and denied ever having seen such a thing.

Dionysius came every year to see us bringing something, usually pears, each time. Occasionally we have visited his house too with its lovely views across the valley. From there, Margarita's olive press is invisible, hidden by a broad barrier of olive trees, but there are two landmarks which are prominent even from such a distance. One is the twelve-foot high dry stone wall holding up the outer edge of the *aloni*, and the other is a ruin, a real ruin, which stands at the back of the olive press. 'A ruin among ruins', as a friend kindly described it. But at a distance, the ruin is the size of a pebble and easily lost in the stone of the hillside. On one visit to Dionysius, I met his son, who was home on holiday from Philadelphia where he owned a distribution business. I asked him if he would like to live here again.

'This is fine for holidays,' he replied, 'but there's not much work here, apart from tourism. I would rather work in the States for much bigger opportunities.'

*

Philoxenia has always been characteristic of Greece. People here show their generosity in many ways. On one occasion I drove Sandra and Daisy to the village and they waited in the car as I went to find Andreas. I didn't expect to be longer than about ten minutes. As they waited they heard a deep and ancient voice singing.

'It's a long way to Tipperary, it's a long way to go...'

A weather-beaten face appeared, smiling, at the open window.

'You English?' he asked.

Sandra said yes.

'It's a long way to Tipperary...' he was singing again.

'I fight with the English in the war,' he said. 'Many good friends and many songs.'

He disappeared and came back a few minutes later with two bunches of basil, one each.

'Welcome,' he said, 'and basil for the memory.'

'You are very kind,' said Sandra.

'Goodbye.' And then, 'Good-bye Piccadilly, good-bye Leicester Square...' he sang, laughed, waved and disappeared.

✻

Making friends here is not difficult. I will not forget one particular dark evening, as I rode down to the *psari* taverna, suddenly a big figure jumped out of the shadows and signalled for me to stop. I recognised the man but didn't know his name; we had exchanged a few words in the past. He pulled out a wallet and showed me a photograph of a gentleman wearing an imposing military cap. I was quite unsure of the correct response; was it politics or family or some other connection? I thought a joke would be the safest reply.

'Mussolini?' I said.

There was a moment of astonished incredulity, then he burst into laughter. For years afterwards we would greet each other with 'Mussolini!' and fall about laughing. The photograph was of ex-King Constantine of Greece, and my friend a stout royalist supporter.

*

Some of the friends we make at random here will come to the house to visit, during the summer when they know that we will be at home. Our second official visitor was James. This was the year that he had brought the mermaids to the taverna, and now he was keen to bring them to the house. I was happy to agree, but imposed two conditions. One, that they should arrive before ten-thirty in the morning, and two, that each visitor should bring her own drinking water. I wondered what the few locals who might have witnessed the scene would have thought, as twenty American girls, in their late teens and early twenties, trailed up the hillside carrying water bottles, sunshades, cameras, binoculars; one wore cowboy boots.

'In case of snakes,' she explained. 'I'm from Texas,' she added smiling sweetly – not a come on, surely; was she hiding an apple?

When they reached the house they explored everything and everywhere. Some were exhausted by the climb and sat drinking their water. Others wanted to try the water from the sterna, which had been treated with purification tablets. They all asked me what it was like to live here.

'Here you have four priorities,' I replied. 'Water comes first. This is why I asked you all to bring your own. Then there's logistics. More than an hour is needed to bring anything here from a local shop; about two hours' return journey for the nearest supermarket, and three hours round trip for the town. All supplies, not just food, have to be planned well in advance. The third factor is systems. There is nothing here, no taps or switches; you have to select and devise all your own domestic systems for lighting, heating, cooling, sanitation, washing. The fourth is why we are here: the panorama. It is one of the most beautiful in the whole Mediterranean. That's just my opinion.' But I did admit there might be another place almost as beautiful somewhere among the other sixteen countries bordering the Mediterranean.

One of the girls, with long golden hair past her shoulders, not the one from Texas, agreed and said she wanted to stay.

'That's not possible,' said James; 'our yacht is due to sail at six tomorrow morning.'

'That's long enough,' she said.

But we all walked down the hill together and had drinks at the taverna, and she returned with the others and sailed or swam away the following morning, just like a good mermaid is supposed to do.

*

In our third summer, the same year that we had invited some good friends of ours from London to visit, the island was engulfed in a great storm on a tropical scale. It started the night before they were due to arrive, with flashes of lightning across the mountains overhead soon developing into blinding white sheets of light over the entire landscape. Thunder rolled from the skies, more deafening than the distant Turkish gunfire that the islanders would have heard on the night Lord Byron died at Messolonghi. It was dark when the first drops of rain fell. Sandra was the one who remembered that our garden seat, which we had hauled up the hill to the *aloni*, was not covered with its plastic rain sheet. Panic increased during the hunt for the sheet, which was eventually discovered at the bottom of a tin trunk. As we raced up the path the rain and the wind were gathering and I wondered whether the seat would be blown over the edge. There was only one trick – persistence – to getting the slightly too small sheet over the seat; had our friends arrived a night earlier, they, no doubt, would have been amused at the sight. We secured the sheet with boulders and raced back to the olive press, where the rain was now pouring off every roof. When we arrived back inside, soaked to the skin, Daisy, then seven and a half, was pleased to see us, and impatient to be missing the action.

'I think I'll have a go on the swing,' she said suddenly.

'But you can't,' we both said simultaneously, and then, in the way that parents often burden their children with the obvious, 'you'll get wet.'

But Daisy had already run out, down the stepped terrace at the front and over to the edge. By the time she reached the swing, her T-shirt and shorts were soaked; she jumped for the ropes, hardly settled herself on the seat and kicked off; the momentum of the swing increased and she rose ever higher to the front and back. Her long hair streamed like the water itself. Intermittent flashes of lightening shot brilliantly through the scene, fixing her motionless on the swing seat while the rhythm of everything else continued to swing, back and forth around her. I remembered the old owner of the olive press and the electric storm that took his wife and daughter. Lightening never strikes twice in the same place; but this wasn't the same place. They were killed by lightning up near the village. Surely, in a way, this was the same place. Let the Greek Gods be judge of that. The swing was reaching now as high as it possibly could. I started to shout, 'Don't…' but didn't know what to say, except to myself about not imposing my paranoia on my daughter. Daisy stopped when she chose to. The storm chose not to.

During the night we were twice awoken by rain beating on the roof and the sound of flooding streams pouring down the steps outside. Our new roof was watertight. At breakfast, the rain eased off and Daisy and I decided to walk down to check that our boat was secure. Daisy wore a swimsuit and I a plastic mac; we both wore plastic bags on our heads and must have made a comical pair. The path was very slippery and the smell of the fresh wet earth like the wet grass of an English lawn, but scented with pine roots and oregano. After ten minutes of slithering and falling over we were both glad to reach the bottom of the hill. Eventually we reached the little freshwater bay where our rubber boat was moored. Everything seemed in good shape, except somebody had put a rope across from their boat to ours. A genial Greek came up saying he owned the other boat. Being about to ask why he had secured his boat to mine, the truth dawned on me. It was my boat that was secured to his and saved from being swept onto the rocks. I wondered if he had managed to get the line across before the sea was really rough; I thanked him warmly and asked him to join me for a drink at the taverna. Only Nionio and Diamanto were around. When I told them that some friends were visiting, Nionio said, 'There will be no more rain today. The weather has changed.'

There was still a damp chill in the air when Daisy and I arrived back at the house, to a most surprising sight. In our absence Sandra had lit an enormous fire in the hearth of the olive press building. Now she was stretched out on a deckchair in front of it and firelight flickered through the room, bringing warmth to bare stone walls.

'We want to give them a warm welcome when they arrive,' she said. 'I'm amazed how easily and quickly this ancient Greek bread oven flares up with just a few bits of paper and kindling. I wish we had one in England; we'd save a fortune on firelighters.'

It brought back memories of summer in Cardigan Bay or the Highlands; it felt as though we should play cards and do a jigsaw puzzle, occasionally venture out in wellies, raincoats and waterproof hats. Trees outside were still dripping when Paul and Margot arrived with their two daughters. Knowing the route from a visit the previous year, they too were surprised to find the three of us slumped in deckchairs before the fire, reading, sleeping and watching the flames dance in the grate. The smoke trailed up against the rear wall and blackened the roof timbers above; black cobwebs hung like mobile stalactites and swayed in the rising currents of warm air. More chairs were pulled up, coffee was made, the children explored inside the house and a typical wet holiday morning at the English seaside was soon forgotten.

By noon it was clear enough to take our guests down to the taverna for some lunch. The feast that day was swordfish, fresh from the early morning after the storm had cleared and therefore firm and moist, unlike anything of the same name which has seen the inside of a cold store. Diamanto had also cooked *fazoulakia*, delicious green beans in tomato sauce. Since Sandra doesn't eat fish, despite vigorous efforts from me to persuade her to, the beans arrived on her plate as a double helping. As usual, Nionio was asleep by the time we finished and I asked Diamanto to put it on the account, which is where all our expenditures at the Taverna now end up. I pay everything at the end of our stay, after laborious adding up which Nionio insists that I do myself. He laughed when I once offered to pay him to add them up, and still refused.

After lunch we were full, and the sun had re-emerged. Under a clear sky we all headed back up to the house. The mountains on Kefallonia loomed high, sharply defined crags and valleys rolling down to a calm sea. The storm had washed away all trace of the mist that sometimes softens the image; now we almost felt that we were one island, joined at the north by mountains. Previous bare patches on the ground were now covered with little bright green shoots sprouting up like new blades of grass. In these spots the ground had been hard, brown and dusty; now the seeds had got the message of spring, of rain and warmth, and had responded immediately. It was a sight both miraculous and sad. None of them could possibly survive a single day of midsummer sunshine without water. Two days later the ground was again hard, brown and dusty. And the new shoots were gone.

13

Garden and stars
Politics, war, sex, arts and gardening; is there anything else?
Love; is there anything else?

The greenest, coolest, wettest spot on the island is on the East coast. It is a garden centre, run by Nikos and his wife, who work all day and talk about plants to customers or anyone else who'll listen. Our visits there taught us how to build a hillside garden, which plants can survive drought, where best to plant oleanders. The flowerbeds here are watered through an intricate maze of pipes, reaching the farthest corner of the garden. On our first visit, we wondered what business we could have in a well-watered garden when we had neither garden nor water; but all over Greece, people with no land create wonderful gardens in empty olive oil tins and terracotta pots on windowsills and balconies.

'Many plants live through the long summer months without water,' Nikos explained. 'The biggest problem is getting them started and some watering is usually necessary in the first summer. Look at these oleanders.'

We had already noticed them, stretching in a broad column, more than fifty yards of pink, white, yellow, purple.

'Once they are established, they get all the water they need during the winter. You must have seen them planted by roadsides and motorways. They get no special watering. Be careful though: the leaves and flowers are very poisonous. If you want a climber to train up on wires against the wall of your house, a good choice is the bougainvillea, which came to Europe from the Amazon.'

He showed us what he called the original bougainvillea, which have acrylic, almost chokingly bright purple flowers, and long spiky thorns.

'You'll see many on houses beside the road leading up to the mountains. Most of the older ones are purple, but now there are plenty of other colours too.'

He showed us softer versions in scarlet and pink and white, and various combinations of the three. We chose one with pale pink petals. And we hoped it would be sturdy enough to enjoy its new home.

For Sandra, who is a far better gardener than I, the purchase of our small pink bougainvillea was symbolic. It was our first attempt at gardening in Greece, creating new life on our land where there had been none before. We decided to put it next to the double doors of the olive press, where there is a small crescent of earth and good shelter. Years ago there had once been a vine there, according to Dionysius across the valley. It had been trained up against the wall and was supported on wires over the terrace, deepening the shade cast by the olive tree. By the end of summer the fruit would be ripe and Dionysius remembered being given sweet dark bunches of grapes, fresh from the vine, as a child. In winter when the leaves had fallen, sunlight returned to the terrace, shining through the bare branches of the vine, and was welcome.

We now faced the practical, if less romantic, challenge of how to water plants in our absence. Nikos said that bougainvilleas need a little watering, from time to time, until the end of the first summer and through the autumn months. Given that we were soon due to leave, this was the first problem. The solution was to buy the ceramic cones used in Austria and Southern Germany for the automatic watering of window-boxes. Bavaria must surely hold the world's gold medal for the magnificent extravagance of its window-boxes and most of these are now watered automatically with cones. When the cone becomes dry, a valve opens to release drops of water until the humidity increases and the valve closes again. I put a 75-litre plastic container on the *pithi* behind the double doors and ran a small bore pipe through the door to connect with the cone, which I buried in the crescent of earth that was to sustain our bougainvillea until the following spring.

*

Zakynthos is always green. In August, when the fields are dusty brown and the grain has long been harvested, the hardy evergreens endure. But in spring, possibly more glorious even than springtime in England, the gardens of Greece are a riot of colour, and the mountains of the Ionian unsurpassed. The following year I experienced a Greek spring for the first time. I returned with Sam and Karen, who were to help me build a new wooden floor in the middle house. The job was too disruptive to be done during the summer vacation period, but Sandra understandably expressed a degree of disbelief that the proposed visit at the end of April should be grandly called 'a business trip'. That spring I was delighted to discover that our bougainvillea had survived and also that the promised garden of our dreams already existed – a natural garden of wild flowers was crowding the mountainside from the olive press down to the sea.

The cypresses and evergreens on the hillside are fresher in spring than in the hot summer months. Silvery olives planted near the mule track are just as they always were, but are now rooted firm in a mountain that is ablaze with colour. Lower fields lie under feathery green barley and randomly seeded bright red pools of poppies. Looking below knee-high grasses is like looking into the sea bed through a snorkel mask; tiny flowers grow close to the roots of taller plants in purple and gold. Each turn of the path up the hillside brings a new flood of colour, which with a little shaping could challenge a rainbow. In the ten-minute walk from the road to the house, you could pass more than a hundred flowering plants; if you are knowledgeable about wild flowers, it may take you a day to reach your destination.

Pink or white shrubs from the cistus family reach all over the hillside and grow in their hundreds along the road from the *micro nisi* to the village. They have a fine, tough, beautiful quality; I think of them as the wild roses of Greece. Great bushes of yellow spartium give off a strong vanilla fragrance and thrive closer to the *psari* taverna, scenting all the air around. The Greeks call these *sparto*, we know them as broom. In the early morning little pink trumpets of convolvulus can be seen every-where, opening in the sunlight. Fragrant white or yellow honeysuckles grow in several places near the house, sharply defined little saxifraga cling to cracks in the rocks. Wild garlic, *umbelliferae*, a shorter version of cow parsley, chrysanthemums and white bell-shaped campanula carpet the hillside so thickly in white, that at a glance, you might even think there had been a fresh fall of snow.

According to Greek legend there are two flowers that are more special to the Gods than the others. The wild carnation, with its feathery red petals, is known as Dianthus, the flower of Zeus. The anemones, which every year announce the beginning of spring, are said to be the footsteps of Adonis walking free from the underworld to be with Aphrodite, his love. On our hillside they are white and purple. Elsewhere the ornithogalum grows freely and is known as the Star of Bethlehem, for its star shaped petals and yellow centres. Everywhere the natural beauty of the spring inspires myth and folklore.

Behind the little house there is a tiny field of lilies that flower in spring, creamy white and brilliant when the sun is out. Sam was the first to see them between two stone walls. Every stem carried seven or eight perfect blooms and buds that would soon open. I remembered an image in one of the most beautiful lines of modern Greek poetry by Vrettakos – the vision of a lily being presented to a lover, as a mere stalk might attach to an Evening Star.

Sam picked one for Karen and there were still twenty lilies left, with nobody to accept them.

All the flowers attract wild bees and butterflies. The butterflies are magical, flying wherever they choose, changing direction and back again, apparently without concern either for the past or the future. You can watch pairs of butterflies dance around each other, freely moving apart and re-pairing, spiralling upwards with effortless freedom. Scientists may say otherwise, but I for one cannot predict the flight of a butterfly, unlike birds, which mostly seem to have a flight path in mind when they leave the African continent for the eaves of our house in Suffolk, or one branch for another. Purpose creates and destroys but purposelessness does neither, except by accident, and I think not in the flight path of a butterfly. While the wild flowers are free to be where they are, the butterflies are free to be where they are not, or where they are, or in between; it doesn't matter. There are so many colours and movements, sudden silences and stillness. Wings clasped together on a flower and a slow wide opening to feel the sun and show a greater brilliance. Disappearance in a flash proves the show is not for you. I personally don't want to know their names, their habits and their habitats and would rather hear myths and fairy tales, or just return to this hillside in the spring and watch.

*

One morning Sam asked me to take him on a tour of our land. So we spent the morning walking, discussing when to harvest almonds, which were the best shady places to rest, the most fruitful trees. We have two large almond trees that cast welcome shade in the afternoon. Fresh green almonds can be harvested in the late summer, though by this time the trees themselves look quite unhappy with the heat, their leaves shrivelled. At the end of winter, before other trees feel the coming of spring, the almond trees display their white and pale pink blossoms. On a bright morning in January or February, against a blue sky and the grey stones of the olive press, the almond branches sway lightly in the wind, as though tossing the winter months behind them. Outside the window of our bedroom is a smaller almond tree, which seems almost to die in summer, only to bloom again each spring. Light sprays of pink blossom open in the breeze and the slender trunk and branches bend and sway, as young trees do, in gentle currents of air, beneath open bedroom windows.

The way through to what we now call the garden is at the shady end of the little house. Once an ancient fig tree grew here, which fell in a winter storm and has now been replaced by a young fig tree that has grown up from the same roots. The branches, which are sparse and open, carry bright green leaves and shade the far corner of the roof, until overtaken by the stronger shade of the almond. The figs are seldom ripe to eat by the time we leave each summer and I like to think that Margarita harvests them herself. Beside a low stone wall there are thick clumps of soft furry leaves, more like the long silvery ears of grey rabbits. Beyond is a terrace stretching to the far edge of the garden, completely flat and guarded, it would seem, by a ten-metre high cypress tree, which shades most of the terrace during the afternoon. This is an ideal site for pitching a tent, which our children enjoy as their own base away from the main part of the house. The hot morning sun strikes this spot without relief in summer, so even teenagers choose not to lie in after eight o'clock.

The garden ends where stone walls converge. Smooth depressions in the rock indicate the spot where a makeshift seat would once have been. A length of cypress trunk is now once again creating the perfect place from which to admire the view. The people before us here knew the best places to sit and rest and look out over the landscape and the sea. Here we learn, not teach. Sam had sent us from Thailand a large brightly painted and varnished sun-shade, with scarlet hibiscus flowers and mythical crested purple birds. It now provides lovely shade for the sunny side of the garden seat. Though when I placed it, I did wonder whether our predecessors, no doubt good members of the Greek Orthodox Church, would have approved of the Buddhist transformation of the top of the garden.

The back of the olive press is the only place where you can look up and see the sea directly above the ridge of the roof, below the horizon and the sky. The roof masks the entire landscape down to the coast, shortens the distance to the sea and my olive press becomes a fisherman's house. Beyond here, our land rises steeply to a circular threshing field, our *aloni*. A vertical stone wall twelve to fifteen feet high supports the front, gradually declining to join the hill on the far side and complete a semi-circle. The great structure can be seen from the next headland and out at sea. From the coast or the other side of the valley Margarita's olive press is virtually invisible. Built into the hillside and well camouflaged against marauding Turks or unwelcome visitors from Algiers, only the *aloni* wall risks giving everything away. Unlike the stone walls of the houses, its great dry stone wall has no protection from the prevailing winds and autumn gales and no roof for shelter from the penetrating storms of winter.

The *aloni* was last used as a threshing field in the early 1940s, though the field is as level now as when it was created two hundred years ago. In true Greek style, only the front half belongs to us, though we have put a garden swing seat under the shade of trees at the back, with apologies to the owner of the rear half. From here the panorama is 180 degrees, but feels like 360 for the unmathematical. In the whole expanse the farmhouse in the next valley is the only building to be seen. The rest is landscape, coastline and sea. Little boats seemingly take hours to cross the great wide sea. On such a vast canvas, the *micro nisi* is no longer dominant.

Within five minutes walk of our *aloni* there are three others, indicating the agricultural wealth that used to bless this area; there is another beautiful *aloni* a little way down the mule track, quite small and surrounded now by almond trees; this one is also a perfect circle, covered in the spring with fresh green grass and later with brown and saffron sprays. Grain must have been planted on very steep slopes to justify investment in five *alonia* here, unless each farmer wanted his own threshing capacity.

Iannis had marked all his olive trees with his initials 'IS'. With a small pot of red paint, I changed the markings on ours to 'PS'. 'Podi', pronounced 'Rodi', is my Greek name.

*

You live here as though absorbed by nature. The sky, the sun, the sea, the land, all is changeable in the seasons and in time. Only the stars are constant. One evening, as sometimes happens in the summer, we experienced such a fierce electric storm that there was no counting between lightening flashes and thunder for almost half an hour. Sam calculated that during the storm sixty litres of water had been collected in the *sterna*. This was based on one centimetre's depth of water being the equivalent to approximately fifteen litres. Fortunately no damage was done, apart from to some wild flowers that Karen had picked and left on the terrace for pressing. The one rule for pressing flowers, I understand, is to keep them dry.

Regardless of the dramas of the night, the sun emerges every morning, more like a returning moon, silver and cool, a bright colourless rim, a crescent scimitar cleaned and polished from the day before. The sun seems never to change its colour or move so quickly as in the first steep climb from the horizon. For those who also like the sunset, there is temptation to travel half-way round the island, westwards, to a popular spot on cliff-tops a hundred feet above the sea. The sunsets there are always magnificent, although if you know the story, the deep purples and reds which flood to stain the sky and sea, are reminders of the tragic slaughter over these cliffs, during the Greek civil war, half a century before. One group of islanders outnumbered another, and fought them back to the cliff tops and beyond; there were no survivors. Now every sunset is a commemoration.

In the sunrise and the sunset, the bright new dawn or the peaceful sinking into night, there is a paradox. For Europe, the sun rises in the old world and sets in the new. But would the sun not be better coming from the new world than the old? When Odysseus commanded his last great voyage, described not by Homer, but in the Inferno by Dante, he followed the sun. For new experience of an un-peopled world, beyond the pillars of Hercules, he sailed on, into the Atlantic, towards a great mountain island and fatal shipwreck. Few have dared to enter the domain of the greatest Greek poet and stand comparison, and nobody has described better than Dante such driving, manic, energy to reach beyond the sunset.

The *aloni* is the place from which to see the night. Shadows from the mountain cover the olive press in the late afternoon or evening depending on the hour of sunset and the season. The skies above the mountain often send messages with the clouds, to tell us that the sun is sinking in the sea beyond the western coast of the island. Night comes faster than the day, the stars emerge from where they always were and more quickly than the morning sun. One night Sandra and I lay on the long soft grasses of the *aloni*, looking up at the stars. There was nothing between the night sky and the earth except for us; darkness and space was the night, but not between us. It was the joining of the Southern Cross and the North Star. The earth was too far away for us to notice whether or not it trembled. Perhaps.

A brilliant slice of light falls through the sky. A falling star. All over the world, children ask where they go. The answer is here over the mid-sea darkness, on the waves. If you are not over the age of eight, or not qualified in astronomy, you can see the shower of fallen stars that are caught by fishermen. They hold them in glittering glass bowls, just above the surface of the sea, to attract the fish. Before daylight, the fishermen must release their stars or they themselves dissolve. Their boats, their nets, hooks, lines, weights, oars, anchors, everything disappears. Before the darkness ends, the fishermen must set free the stars to float a moment on the water and sink, transforming at a greater depth into friendly creatures of the sea, silvery fish sometimes, or mermaids.

14

AHI !

Even roots burn at the heart of the fire. But not stone

We were swimming in the green transparent waters of the far beach. Later we learned that it was the afternoon of the tenth of August, but who cares about the date? Most of the people there wouldn't have known it either. It was also the night of the new moon. Almost nobody knew that, at four in the afternoon. But there was one thing, noticed by us all, that was unmistakable; a gradual darkening of the skies beyond the cliffs to the north-west, and the smell of smoke.

As we swam, a few small white flakes of ash began to fall into the sea.

'A fire in the mountains,' said Sandra. Then she laughed. 'Pompeii could have started like this.'

I swam slowly back to the beach, paused to find flip-flops and walked over the shingle to the steep slope of the road. Both the smell and the smoke were a little thicker here. High up in the mountains to the north-west I could see smoke blooming out from the hillside, somewhere below the summit of the range, far away from the olive press. But the winds in Zakynthos are often unpredictable and easily change direction. I decided to drive back.

On the road that led around the mountain, a number of people had collected to watch the fire smoking in the distance. Nionio's daughter,

Katerina, was one of them.

'Don't worry,' she said, 'it's a long way from your house, and from ours at the top.'

Occasional flames could now be seen amid the smoke.

'It will soon die down,' she said.

I returned to the beach and reassured Daisy and Sandra. The fire was too far away to do any harm. We swam and lazed around for at least another hour and then went to the fish taverna. Nionio had his binoculars out.

'It's a big fire,' he said. 'I'm surprised they haven't called out the planes.'

A few minutes later a spotter plane could be seen flying slowly over the central area of the fire. Within half an hour a roar overhead made everyone look up to see the enormous yellow carcass of a fire service plane level out over the taverna, drop down to the surface of the sea and scoop up gallons of precious water for the fight on the hillside. It rose up, circled once and flew low through the smoke, to disgorge a deluge of sea into the heart of the fire. A diffusion of steam exploded and we all let off a tremendous cheer. Then, as we watched, in keen and steady anticipation of another victory, the plane changed course. It flew for a few minutes in the direction of mainland of Greece and was gone.

Everybody looked at their watches, and then again at the fire. This was the end of the working day.

'What, no overtime?' I said, only half joking. The water may have had some effect at the origin but the slow advance down the mountain-side continued.

'No need to worry,' said Nionio. 'It's nowhere near your house.'

I was glad to agree with him.

After another drink, we left the taverna for the evening walk up the hill. In the dusk Margarita's olive press looked serene and magical through the olive cypress trees that camouflage her so well.

'You're quite safe,' I whispered. 'No need to worry.'

The activities continued as usual. Sandra sorted through a few things. Daisy started her shower. My main concern was for Dionysius across the valley. Walking up the hill, we had seen a fire engine beside his house and flames licking into bushes and olive trees above the road. I soon put on long trousers, gathered up some gardening gloves and said to Sandra that I should go over to see if he needed any help. He would certainly do the same for me, were he not now in his late seventies! I started down the path to the road, then stopped. Higher up on our own hillside a great grey billowing ball of smoke filled the sky. No more worrying about Dionysius, I must stay here. I turned and walked up the mule track towards the smoke. High above our olive press, I left the track and entered a small field leading down into the valley. Smoke was belching up over the far edge. I walked towards it. Here I could see nothing, but the sound, which I had never heard before, was unmistakable. Crackling, rustling, running, sparking, splitting laughter. Stay where you are and you'll burn. When I turned I hadn't yet seen a single flame close by. The fire was still beyond the edge.

Back at the olive press, I found Sandra up on the *aloni*; she had been very worried and was glad to find that I hadn't gone off to help Dionysius. I told her that the fire was now on our hillside.

'I know that.'

Our arms reached round each other for a moment.

'I must go down and put some things in a bag,' she said.

By now, smoke was pouring over the *aloni* and again I heard the fluid rustle of fire. Suddenly bushes marking the far boundary of our land burst into a sheet of flame. I turned and saw the blaze reflected in the end wall of the olive press. Time to go. I went down to the house where Daisy was still wet from her shower.

'We must leave now,' I said.

Sandra, in that short time, had gathered up in a holdall everything that we needed for the evening. We locked all the doors and set off down the path. The second olive tree we passed had already caught and flames were reaching up the trunk. Beyond it, the steep downward slope on the far side of the path was ablaze; olive trees which had been caught were flaming high like roman candles, hollow trunks acting like chimneys.

The wind brought burnt and burning debris towards us. Hands over your ears, shut your eyes and the smell alone would tell of the approaching disaster. All over the hillside, where the front line of the fire had passed, olive trees and cypresses were left blazing. Far up the mountain slopes where it had all begun, torches were alight, flaming into the night sky. Watching from the coast of neighbouring Kefallonia, you might have thought it a celebration.

By now nothing could be done, except get out of the way and pray.

Further down the path we heard the first olive tree as we passed, crack, crack again and fall, showering the surrounding dried up grass with sparks and burning twigs. As we turned to look, Sandra said, 'If we'd left ten minutes later, we couldn't have used the path. We'd have been scrambling over stone walls, with only the flames to see by.'

The lower part of the path was some distance from the fire so we reached the car without further difficulty and drove down to the taverna. Nionio expressed his concern by producing ouzos all round; Daisy began to relax, Sandra still looked worried. And I knew I had to go back. The hammock, the swing, the chair on the *aloni*, all were vulnerable. Most importantly, not all the window shutters were closed. The sooner it were done the better, and the ouzo helped. I said I had to go back; I also said it in Italian, generally addressing three or four of my Italian friends who were sitting at nearby tables. There were no offers to help. I wished my Italian friend Alberto, Napoleonic Alberto, had been there. He would have rounded up, in no time, half a dozen of his fellow countrymen and had them marching up the hill with buckets and spades. Nionio's drinking companion at the time, an Irishman called Stuart, came over shaking an almost empty bottle of ouzo. 'I'll help,' he slurred. 'You're very kind,' I replied, 'I may ask for help later,' imagining him panting up the hill like a salamander and ending in a puff of smoke.

The fire had still not reached the lower slopes, but higher I had to leave the path and climb over stone walls to reach my olive press. Everything else around was burning but as yet nothing had touched the walls. I went up twice to the *aloni* to collect the cushions and frame of the garden seat, then I gathered in the hammock and the swing, and finally closed all four shutters. Fortunately there was nothing else that could be done. 'Goodbye, lovely olive press, I'll be back in the morning.' As quickly as possible I climbed down over walls, skirting fallen olive trees and blazing shrubs. When I reached the road, I saw that the fire had got there first.

A fire-engine was in action, hosing torrents of water at the trees and shrubs by the edge of the road, to prevent the fire from engulfing the car, which I had left in the usual place. Already sparks had come through the window and burnt the front seat; ash covered the whole of the outside. Sandra told me later that she had put the bag of passports, money, cheques and tickets in the front pocket of the car, for safety. I drove it off quickly and the fire engine moved on.

Another ouzo was waiting at the taverna and Sandra, Daisy and I discussed what we should do next. We thought that friends of ours, Johnny and Vanessa, who ran the Pelligoni sailing club and taverna, might have a spare room for tonight and in the morning we could consider the options. Meanwhile I wanted to go back and ask the firemen if there was anything they could do. We drove back up the track, to the place where the car had nearly melted with our most important worldly goods. Many fire engines and firemen were there. Sirens screeched.

'Where is the captain?' I asked.

Soon a man appeared, in his early forties, with three stripes on his shoulders.

'Why is there no aeroplane working to help stop this fire?'

'It's too late now; they've gone home.'

'My home is in the middle of that fire.'

'We can't use planes close to houses. If the water were to hit the roof the whole house could be destroyed.'

'What are you going to do then?'

'We'll come and look, to see if we can help. Climb into the fire-engine and show us where to go.'

I told Sandra what was happening and clambered into the front of the enormous fire engine. I didn't like the idea of being at the house for the third time that evening in the midst of fire, but it was better to be with Greek professionals than absent Italian tourists.

We drove up through the little village to the top of the mountain, turning into the narrow dead-end track that led to Giorgos' house. We were five hundred metres above Margarita's olive press. I reassured the captain, that last summer a water lorry had succeeded in turning round in Giorgos' garden. The fire engine looked about twice the size of the water lorry but somehow it managed to turn around in the garden without apparent damage to chickens, dogs, olive trees, or Giorgos himself, who seemed pleased to be getting such service from the fire brigade. I led them down the rocky mule track, which was more than usually hazardous in the dark. At the point where the fire had crossed the path, we met Giorgos' wife, near to hysteria. The firemen could do nothing about her. We had our own problems. Olive trees were burning beside the track; trunks and branches were cracking; we were descending into hell. In the field on the left, two trees crashed to the ground simultaneously. We were quite close to the olive press by now. I presumed the firemen behind me knew what they were doing and would know if it was too dangerous to walk any further down. The blaze ahead looked particularly dense.

'I'll lead now,' said the captain. 'It looks a bit dangerous here. Are we close to your house?'

'Yes, yes, really not far...'

I think they must have been wearing flame-proof clothing. My shirt was already burnt in several places and this last inferno of burning olive trees on both sides of the track would make it worse. There was a sharp pain in the corner of my right eye; then we were through to the path in front of our house, which the flames had not yet reached.

The firemen looked around the house, then I led them up to the *aloni*. The fire had burnt round the back of the *aloni* and was only now beginning to burn the grasses on the threshing field itself.

'We can't do anything here,' they were saying. 'Our hose-pipes are not long enough and this fire will not be stopped by clearing a bit of ground here and there.'

'Your house should be reasonably safe,' said the captain. 'Stone walls and tiled roofs are pretty safe against fire. The only danger is from the two olive trees in the middle and the one at the back. If they catch, they could fall on the buildings, break through the tiles and set fire to the timber structure of the roofs. But it's unlikely.' The captain was reassuring.

'We must go now. Will you show us the way down?'

We all got as far as the first blockage of fallen olive trees on the path when the captain leapt over the wall on his left and started down the field in a direction which was unfamiliar to me.

'Were you with us in Greece during the war against the Germans?' he asked suddenly.

'I'm not old enough, but I would have been.'

He laughed and I pointed out he was going in the wrong direction.

We crossed the mule track again at a suitable point and regained the path down the hill. By now it was easy to follow. The path shone white against the surrounding black; unlike those on either side, the grasses trodden into the pathway had not burnt. Five minutes later we were back at the road and the captain and his men returned to their colleagues and their three fire-engines.

Further down the lane I found Sandra and Daisy at the car.

'My darling,' said Sandra, 'we went back to the top to find you.'

'But we couldn't and Mum was so worried,' said Daisy, reaching for my hand. 'And she was driving on the wrong side of the road.' I looked at Sandra. 'It was really dark and we'd been looking for you and when we went round a hairpin we had to swerve off into the mountain to avoid a truck. It had really bright headlights.'

'Good job you weren't on the other side,' I said.

'We couldn't find you,' said Sandra softly.

I gave them both a big hug.

'That sounds like the most dangerous part of the evening.'

We decided to drive over to Pelligoni. It was about ten o'clock when we arrived and many people were still eating and drinking at the bar. Johnny and Vanessa were chatting and gave us their usual warm welcome. Yes, we could certainly sleep on mattresses in the room which they used as an office.

Sleep wasn't easy.

'You mustn't hope that we can escape a fire like that,' said Sandra.

'I have to hope, and we might. The firemen said there was a good chance.'

'But not if the olive trees in the middle catch...'

'No, not if they catch. Darling, what do people put in a bag, if they have to leave suddenly?'

She said it was easy with so little time. Passports, tickets, money, a change of clothes, contact numbers. Harder with more time.

'No sentimental decisions about pictures and souvenirs?' I asked.

'No time for that,' she said. 'You went back for the hammock. Risked your life for a hammock!'

'My life wasn't at risk and I had to go back anyway for the shutters.'

'And if we had already closed them?'

'Let's go to sleep.'

None of us slept well that night.

I decided to go up to the house early the following morning.

'Shall I come with you?' asked Sandra.

I hesitated. 'I think it'd be better if you came on the next visit.'

'Okay,' she said. 'Be careful.'

I drove up our lane and left the car where it had so nearly come to grief the previous evening. To begin with, the path up the hill showed no sign of fire damage, but as I climbed round a bend in the path, a smouldering burnt out battlefield confronted me, ranging as far as I could see. All the way up the mule track olive trees had fallen. The first tree, where we used to rest for shade and water during hot walks, was circled by a ring of white ash, severed limbs of branches lying all around. But you cannot destroy the tree through its branches. Fires go for the trunk, to use it as a chimney and burn down to get the roots. Some trees were still burning at the roots two weeks later, with branches holding onto their green leaves only just beginning to wilt. Many burnt out olive tree trunks glowed red and gave out tremendous heat. Smoke and flames were coming from at least a dozen trees in the immediate landscape. I climbed up over stone walls and terraces, skirting round smouldering olive trees and leaving ghostly white footprints on charcoaled grasses. Finally, I reached Margarita's olive press – our olive press.

I stopped. Green olive trees, cypresses and the carob, still stood, in a close circle around the buildings. Like the first time, some cicadas were singing. The pale stone of the house stood out as it may have done when it was first built, hundreds of years before. All looked exactly as it had on my first solitary visit there, eleven years before. Margarita's olive press was untouched. The central olive trees had not caught. The burning had stopped as it reached the stone walls of the house. Long grasses on the path in front were waving gently, moved by the breeze that always rises here.

*

The rest of the morning was spent hauling water from the *sterna* and carrying buckets to trees where smoke and flames were still active. I knew it was too late to save any of them, but at least it reduced the chance of the fire starting up again, assuming the bastard could find anything more to burn. Five out of our nine olive trees had fallen.

A while later I thought I heard a cry from way down the hillside. Moments later I was sure. A wail carried up from below on the wind: Ahi! From the heart Ahi! Ahi! Ahi! A white shawl and blouse over a dark blue skirt; it was Margarita. Ahi! I couldn't see her face until she climbed up over the last wall, ignoring my outstretched hand to help her.

'Ahi! My olive trees! My olives...'

This was no time to dispute the ownership of fallen trees. The tragedy was there, whoever owned it; whatever the documents said, we both did.

I said something about getting a power-saw to start clearing the trees that had fallen along the track, but Margarita insisted that this was a job for the agricultural guards.

'I'm going to get them,' she said, hoisting herself over the wall at the end of the house. There she hung her head at further scenes of destruction.

'There has never been a fire here before. Never. Never.'

And without goodbyes she walked away up the hill which she knew so well, for better or for worse, and for much longer than most. That was the last time I saw her. Margarita died the following year – strong, impossible, generous, indomitable Greek countrywoman.

Two days following the fire, apparently after endless discussions and phone-calls to the family, Maria agreed to sell us the last remaining part of the house. After ten years of negotiation, we certainly had something to celebrate, which we did, with a Greek party.

Then she changed her mind. Or one of the family changed it. Progress of a kind, perhaps. We had, at least, enjoyed a party...

15

Maria's Sailor
If at last you don't succeed. Go back to the sea

The olive press survived the fire and stood as it had for the last three hundred years. Up at the village, in Iannis' shop, everybody was talking about it and nobody could remember a fire like it.

'You should phone Maria,' said Iannis. 'Tell her that her house is safe.'

I remembered that it was Dionysius who had first introduced me to Maria in the taverna, on one of my earliest visits. She had just then arrived from Athens. We talked about the Olive Press and her house at the front of it. Then she told me that in a former life I had fallen in love with the olive press! As a sailor shipwrecked on the shore, she said, I had climbed up the hill and found shelter there. Then she put a difficult question.

'Do you believe that?' she asked.

At this time Dionysius was still interpreting for me. There's a good Italian phrase –'*Ci credo. Ci credo*' (I believe it. I believe it) and it means, of course, quite the reverse. We agreed it might be prudent to be more ambiguous.

'Can you believe something about yourself for which you have no memory or evidence?'

'I believe it,' she said, and that settled it.

She knew I wanted to buy her house with its ugly tin roof over the kitchen. She refused to sell, every time I mentioned it. The year after the fire, I telephoned her in Athens, as I had done almost every year for twelve years. 'Patience,' she replied.

After twelve years? I wrote her a letter, 'You told me the story of a sailor once,' I reminded her. 'Any more patience and I will go back to the sea and return to buy your house in another life,' I continued. 'Now, after so many years, I will offer you another half million drachmas to cover additional costs.' This was then an extra thousand pounds, a persuasive blend of the poetic and the commercial, I considered. Finally, I added the thought that if she didn't sell now I might soon give it all away to the children and it would be a long time before she had another offer. A further blend perhaps – carrot and stick.

Within a month Lambis telephoned me. 'Maria is coming to town with her sisters Kali and Doula. She wants to sell!' I was in disbelief. How could it end so quickly? Something would go wrong. 'The bad news,' Lambis went on, 'is that she wants to finish it now, in three days, before her brother Giorgos arrives. It's completely unrealistic.' We agreed to get an engineer's site plan and leave Maria to solve problems with her brother. Better to bring into the open now any rights he may have in the matter, rather than risk litigation later.

All was rearranged for the following month and when I arrived, Lambis gave me a small brown paper package, a present from Maria. It was a small red hardback book, a Bible, published by Jehovah's Witnesses, in English.

'She's a firm believer,' he said.

'Is this an invitation to convert, before the deal is done?' I asked

'You know, I have come to like the three sisters. They're good people, kind and with integrity. They would have been good looking when they were young; now they are old. You will be shocked by Kali. She's very ill and must get back to Athens to the hospital as soon as possible.'

The following morning I went apprehensively to the public notary's office. Surely such a long project cannot end so easily? I remembered the first time, when had we only just prevented Margarita from walking out. This may be even worse. There were three of them! I had come straight from the bank with enough cash to pay the tax and puff out my pockets embarrassingly. Nobody followed me in the street. Lambis was already at the office talking to Tasos, the pale-faced lawyer who would be creating the contract. He used a manual typewriter, on which he had drafted our last three contracts. On the other side of the room a large woman chain-smoked and churned out documents at high speed from a modern computer terminal.

A shuffling sound at the door announced the arrival of the three sisters. Kali, dressed entirely in black, was being supported between the other two, her face yellowish and her hands shaking. She was put on a chair near the door and I went over to greet her.

'I'm very pleased to see you again, and hope you will soon be better.'

Nobody said what her illness was; was it cancer?

'Welcome,' she whispered and smiled piercingly.

Maria came over and we shook hands.

'Welcome.'

She looked the eldest of the three. A friendly smile crinkled the corners of her dark brown eyes. She wore a long green woollen jacket, too warm for the day's temperature.

'Thank you very much for the book.'

'You will find it interesting, I think.'

'No religion or politics,' I could hear Lambis murmuring.

We all sat down, waiting for something to happen. Lambis said we should go off to pay the tax, leaving Maria and Kali with Doula, who had also come over to greet me.

At the tax office, an overall value was established, in line with our own calculations.

'You are not buying a palace then,' said the cashier.

Back at the notary's office we encountered bad news. The room was now seething with people demanding to transact their legal affairs. Our own contract could not be done before tomorrow. The three sisters were shocked and distressed. Not only had they booked seats on the bus back to Athens, but Kali concerned them more. She was weaker; time was passing and she needed to return to hospital as soon as possible. Another worrying problem was their large plastic bag of fresh lamb from the village, which needed to be stored somewhere cool, in order to be in fair condition when they reached home. Lambis and I helped the sisters leave the notary's office and walk to a small hotel nearby where Kali was immediately carried off to bed and then the other two discussed the best location for the meat.

In the afternoon, I hired a car and drove along the new coast road to the north of the island. I parked at the bottom of our hillside. There were no clouds. The dark sea was calm, untouched by even a light breeze. This was a summer's day, but at the beginning of November. There had been rain and more was forecast, but for now this was holiday weather without the tourists, or anyone else. The roads and the taverna were deserted. A few people could be seen gathering olives, but our hillside was quiet. I trod carefully through delicate pink cyclamen and sturdy autumn crocuses, not the overwhelming wild-flower display of springtime but wonderfully unexpected at the end of autumn. Everything was freshly green and the path overgrown. The first thing I saw when I reached the little hamlet was the broken wall of Maria's kitchen and the partially collapsed door. I decided that if the parts were daunting, look at the whole; and vice versa I suppose. Inside I checked the level of the *sterna* – good and high. Everything needed a clean, but otherwise all was well.

I looked again at Maria's house and wondered at the near impossibility of putting a value on it. She had spent her childhood there with her sisters and her brother Georgios. It was a wonderful place for children, just fifteen minutes walk from the sea. They would have had goats and chickens, perhaps cats. They would have gathered almonds and helped with the olive harvest and travelled on mules, when their parents allowed. After they were grown up they returned to visit from time to time. Their mother was the first to die and their father lived there until his death thirty years ago. Maria was holding on to her memories. Giorgos was more interested in cash. He wanted to buy from Maria and sell to me at two or three times the real value. He and the other three sisters owned land further down the hill. He tried to persuade Maria not to sell the house unless I also bought the land. We had discussions about it for many years. It would have been an expensive *hors d'oeuvre* to the main dish, I thought, as I locked up.

Lambis had warned me to expect a claim by Maria for more drachmas to cover extra expenses and driving back I rehearsed the arguments. I too had incurred extra expenses, not least on this visit. In the letter I had offered extra drachmas to cover expenses which Maria had accepted. We had also agreed a price for the house almost twice the value set by the tax office. Plenty there for additional expenses. A lorry braked sharply in front. I was back to reality, and a sore neck.

When we next met at the office, I said I felt like a mule heavily laden with drachmas. Most of them smiled, even Kali. The contract was a combined output from Tasos on the typewriter and the chain-smoking lady with the computers. Tasos seemed to be faster. Finally the documents were ready and Maria signed, without trying for a higher price. Poor Kali was dragged to her feet and taken across the room, where the newly stapled document was ready for her signature. There was no chair. Doula released Kali's right arm. She sagged onto the table and somehow managed to sign before being gently hauled back to her seat near the door.

Two lawyers in attendance, one for Maria and one for me, now started to count out the drachmas and pass them to her; she put the bundles into a plastic bag. When all was done, she reached into another bag, pulled out a long iron key, gave it to me and burst into tears. Thank you, I said and gave her a big hug, wetting the side of my face as though I had been the one crying. End of an era. And too late now for a change of heart.

Lambis said I should make a contribution for last night's hotel room and pay the two lawyers. Most of it goes to the lawyers' benevolent fund, he said. So it was drachmas to the public notary and a few each to Tasos and the lady at the computer for cigarettes, no doubt – and drachmas for the engineer who had done the plan. The mule was now unburdened. Later I tried hard to persuade Lambis to take drachmas for all his hard work. He refused emphatically.

'It's friendship,' he said.

'Friendship can't be so one-sided.'

'Think of it as a mortgage then,' he answered, but didn't answer when I asked how to pay off the mortgage.

This was the last episode in fifteen years of buying the houses of Margarita, Iannis and Maria. It felt like an ending. But feelings can be deceptive; it was just a slow beginning.

16

Greek Gift
Give away what you cannot keep or sell

Finally, we had achieved the purchase of Maria's house and now after fifteen years the hamlet known as Margarita's Olive Press was reunited at last. A rare corner of rural Greece, remote from the trappings of modern life now belonged to us. Now, however, after more than a decade of hard work and surprise, a difficult question was threatening; what next? Learn to give away that which you can neither keep nor sell, wrote Machiavelli, and it's good advice; what else could one do, except, I supposed, destroy?

Sandra and I were now both retired. She had left her university early, I am glad to say, having been acting vice-chancellor for her last six months. Neither she nor I wanted to spend the next years with me scrambling around over roofs replacing slipped tiles and restoring fallen beams. So keep, sell, or destroy? When we faced the question it was clear that we would not keep Margarita's olive press, but nor could we sell this part of the last fifteen years of our lives. As for destroying it, fire had nearly chosen this option for us last year and once again I thanked the gods that we were spared such an outcome. We decided to give the house and all of its land to the children. Why not? It was a good solution and had, perhaps, been in my mind from the beginning. As those richer than us know, giving is not such an easy matter. The first thing is to establish whether the potential recipients actually want the gift in question.

In considering how to present this gift of land and sweat and love, I realised that my family would need me to complete one final transaction for them. For years – since the beginning in fact – I had been talking to Iannis about the possibility of buying the empty cottage of his just a hundred metres down from the olive press. It was tiny, with an acre of land directly beneath the lower terrace of the olive press. 'My darling,' Sandra would say, 'you can't possibly buy up all the Greek real estate from here to the sea,' but I remembered my first visit to the hamlet and knew why it was important. I knew generally that it was for sale and if someone else were to buy the land and build on it, our panorama would be ruined. Buying up land all the way to the coast was, of course, not possible, or necessary, because the hillside falls away sharply just beyond Iannis' land. But his part was essential to safeguard the panorama.

Annual discussions with Iannis had previously resulted either in his asking too high a price or just not wanting to sell at any price. Because of the attached land, his price had always been relatively higher than for our other purchases and we didn't now want to put more of our relatively scarce funds into the Greek hillside. But the value of the hamlet would be greatly increased if Iannis' property were included. Then we wondered, what if the children were to buy Iannis' property and agree to let us use it whenever we wanted? We could organise renovation and install the necessary kitchen and shower-room facilities and it would help us find out whether the proposed recipients really wanted the gift of the rest of the hamlet. We would then have a 'granny flat,' a *yia-yia spiti*, as the Greeks might have called it, close by, but far enough away for us not to interfere in whatever was going on behind us, up the hill.

So Lambis and I began a seemingly endless round of discussions about the best way to structure the whole endeavour. We rejected the normal Greek *epikarpia*, usage, approach, which would probably have incurred UK inheritance tax. We also rejected dividing it up among the five children. Alice in Wonderland might have queried the idea of spending fifteen years re-uniting a property only to divide it up again. We considered the option of a trust but rejected it as too complex and expensive. Finally we decided to set up a non-trading limited company with the five children each holding a twenty percent share. I would occupy the director's role just long enough to manage the process until Iannis' property had been purchased by the company, and the olive press building and the rest of the hamlet had been transferred to the children. If I lived for another seven years, there would be no inheritance tax payable – a good incentive to keep me alive, I liked to joke. Lambis offered to look into the Greek implications and I would do the same in Britain.

Several months later, we had set up a company, Iannis and I had agreed a price and paperwork was now the only barrier. We knew this would be time-consuming and after two more months I found myself phoning him from London to apologise for the delay. Could he please, I laughed, find me a peaceful plot in his lovely local cemetery, with a headstone carved, 'Rodney: died from exhaustion with Anglo-Hellenic bureaucracy.' Though it would have been a different story if it had been the volatile Margarita I was facing, Iannis didn't seem to mind the delay and my papers continued to burgeon at an astonishing rate. Where fifteen years ago I had begun with a single sheet of paper headed 'Margarita's Olive Press', the process, now nearly completed, demands not only a file, but a cabinet.

I began at the Foreign Office in London, where we were to jump our first bureaucratic hurdle. Early on I had learnt that all company documents needed official authentication with a Foreign Office 'apostile' prior to translation into Greek. The 'apostile' is confirmation by the Foreign Office that all legal signatures are authentic. Curiously, this is not an authentication of the contents of the papers, although foreign readers could well be forgiven for thinking otherwise. I spent so much time at the Greek Embassy that by the time we came to the document assigning Greek power-of-attorney, the lovely translator offered to translate it for free. My preferred candidate for the attorney was Makis, who years before had helped me to pipe water down to the *sterna*. He was a bee-keeper; he made excellent wine from his own vineyards; he had learned to speak English; he loved poetry and he built houses. He lived in a wonderful house with a tower and observatory overlooking the northern mountains and coastline. What better qualifications could there be for a power-of-attorney, a legal representative, a *nomimo exprosopo*? So our solicitor in London drafted a four-page document, I reduced it to one, 'for ease of translation, you understand...' and all we needed now was a solicitor's signature. Unfortunately he was away on holiday when we returned to get it. I told his colleague that the matter was urgent. He said it always is. He was persuaded to look at the papers and said almost immediately: 'I can't sign that. It's an incomplete document. It doesn't have the man's name on it.'

When he understood that nobody had yet agreed to do it, he said, 'It's very simple. Go to Greece, appoint the man you want, come back, fill in the name on the document and I'll counter sign it, ready for the apostile.' A rather costly Catch-22, since a representative could not be confirmed in Greece, until matters at this end were resolved. I ventured,

'If I sign the document, as it is, would you officially authenticate my signature?' Fortunately, this alternative solution was accepted and the process flourished to an end with the application of impressive signatures and stampings. The Foreign Office also accepted it for their apostile and the Greek Embassy did the official translation. Happily for us, Makis later agreed and his name appeared on the document, to everyone's satisfaction. The following summer, I arrived back at Lambis' house with all the officially translated documentation feeling as though I had completed a marathon. He seemed pleased and warned me of the next marathon – the Greek legal and tax authorities. For this, he said, it might be necessary to pray.

In the first meeting at the public notary's office there were five lawyers on the case, including Lambis, who recommended Spiros to represent us, partly because he spoke Italian. Then there was the notary himself, who appeared at regular intervals to facilitate or divert the work-flow, and his colleague Olga, who frequently emerged from screens of heavy cigarette smoke to bring a lovely sense of humour to the proceedings. Finally there was Anna, who represented Iannis.

The politics of negotiating with five lawyers in a small Greek notary-office was an interesting experience. Talking with Lambis in English, Spiros in Italian and everyone else in Greek was rather confusing. Just as I would begin to grasp the proceedings, Anna would speed on to the next issue, in rapid Greek from her linguistic machine-gun. Taking cover, I prepared a response in Greek. I waited until she had finished and spoke, very slowly and seriously. 'Anna, if you speak to me in Greek will you please...' By now the whole room was silent and Anna seemed on the point of being embarrassed, 'will you please speak slowly and simply.'

The tension was high. Was this foreigner trying to insult the lawyer on the other side? With a friendly smile I finished, 'I know it's difficult for lawyers to speak slowly and simply.' Everybody laughed, including Anna.

This final endeavour was not proving easy. The next sticking-point came at the tax office. Apparently the official map recorded a public road passing the olive press buildings which conferred valuable privileges on the property and potentially a higher rate of tax. This public road was the same rocky path I had not thought worthy of the name fifteen years ago, the very same *dromo* that had made mules our best, and only, form of transport to the house.

'But the road doesn't exist!' I protested. 'Can we get the map changed?'

'No, no. That would need to be sanctioned by the local authority and even then would require visits from surveyors, local politicians, officials from the forestry department...'

The lady in the tax office agreed to think about the problem of officially documented non-existent roads. We returned anxiously several hours later to hear that tax had been assessed at a reasonable level. It was a triumph of common sense over bureaucracy, not such a frequent event these days in Greece or anywhere else.

Having concluded dealings with the tax office, I collected a cheque for Iannis, from the bank, and took it to the notary's office. Lambis looked at it. 'This has also been made out to the tax office!' What a stupid error; another casualty of translation perhaps. The bank would now be closing and the whole affair would have to be deferred, adding yet another day to the process. Spiros and I raced off, hoping we might still be in time to get a new cheque issued. The main entrance to the bank was closed but a side door was opening to let out staff. Meanwhile an old friend of Spiro's stopped on a motorbike and engaged him in a long and amusing conversation. My frustration mounted until at last the jokes came to an end and Spiros got us into the bank, where a new cheque was issued just as the lights around us were being extinguished and all the staff but one had disappeared. Finally back at the notary's office, much authenticating and signing of documents concluded in the exchange of a cheque for one large iron key. We would add this to our previous collection of five and the acquisition of the entire hamlet was complete. This final project had taken me on a lengthy journey through smoky Greek notary offices and complex tax procedures, but at the end of it all, we had set up a company, acquired a *yia-yia spiti*, and a panorama.

*

The following day, I returned to the house with Sandra, Daisy, and the new key. We were all quiet as I put the huge iron key in the lock and turned it for the first time. With some effort we pushed; the door opened; light flooded through onto two large terracotta vessels, once full of olive oil, now covered with a fine lacework of cobwebs. Otherwise the little stone room was empty. I walked to the other side and unbolted two blue shuttered windows. Again, light rushed in, impatient after all these years, and we stood quietly before an incomparable panorama of dark blue sea and sky, merging somewhere certainly but not precisely.

Surrounding land of almond trees and olives, reached a valley of cypress marking the lower boundary, which no longer belonged to Iannis. So many hours in offices; so many discussions and hurdles; I knew it was all worth it when I experienced again the same feelings as I had on opening the doors of the olive press for the first time, so many years ago.

During the following week we replaced tiles on the roof, cleared the lower terrace and brought down the hammock and the garden swing seat. We talked of serving wine and olives to friends here on the lower terrace, beside the *yia-yia spiti*. Lambis of course would be there, Nionio, Iannis and Makis, but not Kali nor Margarita, again, ever, on this hillside. Not Dionysius. He, turning from a glass of wine or water, might have looked around and laughed, 'So, you know how to *prepare la casa*. Pity you haven't finished.' I wondered whether we would still be speaking Italian or would it be Greek now? He might have read lines from our favourite poem of the Italian renaissance:

Quant' è bella giovinezza	How beautiful is youth
che si fugge tuttavia!	Which flies away so fast!
Chi vuol' esser lieto,sia:	Those who want to, then be happy
di doman non v'è certezza.	For tomorrow is uncertain.

Rejoining the other world that evening, Sandra and I went down to Johnny and Vanessa's clubhouse taverna to celebrate. We drank toasts three times for Margarita's olive press; the first was to Dionysius for the past, the second for Lambis and the present and the third to Makis, for the future. Early the next morning we watched the sun rising over the *micro nisi*, a new sunrise blessing Greek islands and their gifts. At this sunrise, three thousand four hundred years ago, one might have seen from here, white sails pass the southern tip of Kefallonia, on course for Troy.

Epilogue

By Daisy Shields

Along with the olive press my father gave us all some advice.

'Enjoy it for a while and then sell,' he said. 'Take away a few thousand pounds each and find your own unique locations; the Dalmatian coast, Eastern Europe, North Africa. Learn enough language, find a café near where you want to be and over a drink, ask if there is a small stone house for sale and a plot of land...'

Until then, I come every summer to our lovely mountain and remember stories of obsession, hard labour and love.

The story ends where Cavafy began. Ithaka is the next island beyond Kefallonia, not visible from the terrace of the olive press, even on the brightest morning.

'As you set out for Ithaka,
hope your road is a long one,
full of adventure, full of discovery.'
Ithaka, C.P.Cavafy